The Tragic Imagination

The Literary Agenda

The Tragic
Imagination

ROWAN WILLIAMS

OXFORD
UNIVERSITY PRESS

OXFORD

UNIVERSITY PRESS

Great Clarendon Street, Oxford, OX2 6DP,
United Kingdom

Oxford University Press is a department of the University of Oxford.
It furthers the University's objective of excellence in research, scholarship,
and education by publishing worldwide. Oxford is a registered trade mark of
Oxford University Press in the UK and in certain other countries

Published in the United States of America by Oxford University Press
198 Madison Avenue, New York, NY 10016, United States of America

British Library Cataloguing in Publication Data
Data available

Library of Congress Control Number: 2016936813

ISBN 978–0–19–873641–7

Printed and bound in Great Britain by Clays Ltd, Elcograf S.p.A.

Series Introduction

The Crisis in, the Threat to, the Plight of the Humanities: enter these phrases in Google's search engine and there are 23 million results, in a great fifty-year-long cry of distress, outrage, fear, and melancholy. Grant, even, that every single anxiety and complaint in that catalogue of woe is fully justified—the lack of public support for the arts, the cutbacks in government funding for the humanities, the imminent transformation of a literary and verbal culture by visual/virtual/digital media, the decline of reading... And still, though it were all true, and just because it might be, there would remain the problem of the response itself. Too often there's recourse to the shrill moan of offended piety or a defeatist withdrawal into professionalism.

The Literary Agenda is a series of short polemical monographs that believes there is a great deal that needs to be said about the state of literary education inside schools and universities and more fundamentally about the importance of literature and of reading in the wider world. The category of 'the literary' has always been contentious. What *is* clear, however, is how increasingly it is dismissed or is unrecognized as a way of thinking or an arena for thought. It is sceptically challenged from within, for example, by the sometimes rival claims of cultural history, contextualized explanation, or media studies. It is shaken from without by even greater pressures: by economic exigency and the severe social attitudes that can follow from it; by technological change that may leave the traditional forms of serious human communication looking merely antiquated. For just these reasons this is the right time for renewal, to start reinvigorated work into the meaning and value of literary reading for the sake of the future.

It is certainly no time to retreat within institutional walls. For all the academic resistance to 'instrumentalism', to governmental measurements of public impact and practical utility, literature exists in and across society. The 'literary' is not pure or specialized or self-confined; it is not restricted to the practitioner in writing or the academic in studying. It exists in the whole range of the world which is its subject-matter: it consists in what non-writers actively receive from writings when, for example, they start to see the world more imaginatively as a result of reading novels and begin to think more carefully about human personality. It comes from literature making available much of human life that would not otherwise be existent to thought or recognizable as knowledge. If it is true that involvement in literature, so far from being a minority aesthetic, represents a significant contribution to the life of human thought, then that idea has to be argued at the public level without succumbing to a hollow rhetoric or bowing to a reductive world-view. Hence the effort of this series to take its place *between* literature and the world. The double-sided commitment to occupying that place and establishing its reality is the only 'agenda' here, without further prescription as to what should then be thought or done within it.

What is at stake is not simply some defensive or apologetic 'justification' in the abstract. The case as to why literature matters in the world not only has to be argued conceptually and strongly tested by thought, it should be given presence, performed and brought to life in the way that literature itself does. That is why this series includes the writers themselves, the novelists and poets, in order to try to close the gap between the thinking of the artists and the thinking of those who read and study them. It is why it also involves other kinds of thinkers—the philosopher, the theologian, the psychologist, the neuro-scientist—examining the role of literature within their own life's work and thought, and the effect of that work, in turn, upon literary thinking. This series admits and encourages personal voices in an unpredictable variety of individual approach and expression, speaking wherever possible across countries and disciplines and temperaments. It aims for something more than intellectual assent: rather the literary sense of what it is like to feel the thought, to embody an idea in a person, to bring it to being in a narrative or in aid of adventurous reflection. If the artists refer to their own works, if other thinkers return to ideas that have marked much of their working life, that is not their vanity nor a failure of originality. It is what the series has asked of them: to speak out of what they know and care about, in whatever language can best serve their most serious thinking, and without the necessity of trying to cover every issue or meet every objection in each volume.

Philip Davis

Contents

Introduction

People's experience of studying Shakespeare at school is by all accounts a bit uneven; but I don't think I am unusual in finding the first encounter with *King Lear* at A-Level something of a watershed moment. It is a play that never loses its capacity to shock. Because it refuses anything resembling a resolution, a message, or a promise of a more obviously reconciled future, it remains for most audiences and readers a paradigm of tragedy. A couple of years later, at university, I found myself listening to the late Donald MacKinnon lecturing on the problem of evil and excoriating any religious or imaginative framework that tried to make messages and learning opportunities and edifying patterns out of atrocious human suffering and the refinements of cruelty, collective and individual, devised by human beings. Another watershed: partly because I recognized the same insistence as we hear in *Lear*: at some point, even the most confident faith (whether in humanity or in God) has to be honest about what is utterly unresolved in human experience, what cannot be made sense of (if making sense means showing why it's a good thing really).

But this leaves the question of how we can speak at all about this unresolved dimension of what we are and suffer as humans. Representing pain and terror and catastrophe is something we do—whether in half-articulate lament or in the intensities of a Shakespearean drama. Thinking about tragic drama or narrative as a human imaginative activity is bound up with thinking about many aspects of language itself: how it manages unwelcome truth, how it articulates its own failure to master extreme experience, and does so, strangely, in ways that generate new knowledge. Thinking about tragedy is studying one fairly central feature of imagination as such—hence my title: we are not simply passive in the face of terror and suffering, because we can *imagine* it, narrate it, make pictures of it that make it an agenda for others and for ourselves. And to say that we are not passive is not to say that the terror and suffering is anything other than what it is, an experience that threatens our capacity to speak at all in a world such as we inhabit. 'Speak what we feel, not what we ought to say': so ends *Lear*. But speaking what we feel, when what we feel is fear, exhaustion, despair, requires a lot from us. That people respond to the challenge or the pressure is a testimony to the depth of the instinct we seem to have of looking for words even in extremity, even when the foundations of intelligible life together in ordered community are being shaken.

So this short reflection on tragic representing and imagining is not an essay about some essentially 'tragic' quality in human existence, about a pervasive unfriendly fate or some similar category. Tragic drama simply assumes that practically unspeakable things happen and that our various political, metaphysical, and religious concordats with reality are as fragile as could be. But this is different from saying that human life is doomed to 'the tragic'; it is simply a recognition that among the things we most urgently need to learn how to speak of without comfortable lying will be failure and pain. And if we try and learn this, through tragic drama among other things, it helps if we continue to think carefully and attentively about what drama makes it possible for us to feel and know. This means thinking about particular dramas as well as the general characteristics that we may identify as making a drama recognizably tragic. With this in mind, I have attempted here to bring abstract discussion back regularly to such particular dramas, old and new. My hope for this book is simply that it will prompt readers and audiences back to the dramas discussed, with at least some new questions about what it is we have come to know when we have seen/shared in the experience of tragic performance.

And, as I have hinted here and there, we need to ask these questions because of the currents in our peculiar contemporary society that make tragic narration and representation less and less welcome: an instrumentalizing and managerial spirit, an anxious shrinking of language into cliché and formula, a nervousness around emotional risk and exposure that is balanced by profound and fluent sentimentality, a desperate not-knowing-how-to-cope faced with a nightmare world of mass atrocity that sits alongside the acquisitive fevers of our economy...I write unashamedly as a theologian with a long-standing interest in literary studies; and the connection is in large part to do with the way in which tragic representation, like religious words and images, is a means of not closing down substantial and deeply difficult areas of our human experience. Tragedy typically leaves questions painfully open, religious language aspires to some kinds of—if not closure, then at least the promise of sense or of reconciliation. As a good deal of this book will argue, the distinction ends up being a lot less tidy. But the point remains: the challenge is not only how we speak without false consolation in a world like this but how we keep our culture alive to the fact that it *is* 'a world like this'. The denial of fundamental dis-ease and non-resolution is an intensifying of our sickness. The tragic imagination resists that denial, not out of pessimism but out of a rather odd confidence that language is not so easily exhausted or defeated. I hope to make a small contribution to this resistance.

1

Handling Danger

The Political Roots of Tragedy

I

The history of critical discussion is packed with attempts to define
tragedy or 'the tragic'. There have been fierce debates about the differences between classical, mediaeval, and modern approaches to
tragic drama or narrative, about whether late modernity is capable of
producing properly tragic literature, about whether there can be such
a thing as an 'absolutely' tragic vision of reality, about whether the
conventional definitions of the genre are innately elitist, patriarchal,
Eurocentric, about whether tragedy is dependent upon or essentially
hostile to a religious sense of the world. Most of these themes will be
around in the chapters that follow. But it may help to begin by looking
at certain features of tragedy as it first appears with a view to setting
some boundaries for fuller discussion.

The word 'tragedy' begins as a term for one specific kind of ritual
drama in Greece which comes into focus during the sixth and fifth
centuries before the Christian era, especially in Athens. Its beginnings
are not all that easy to discern; but as far as we can tell they involve a
development from the formal recitation of a narrative towards a representation of the narrative in dialogue and (limited) action, com-
bined with formal dance and chant performed by a group. The
occasion was the annual festival in honour of the god Dionysos; more
archaic rural celebrations of Dionysos seem to have been adapted
into the public life of the city, and the urban version increasingly came
to be a moment for encouraging—through competition—the innovative presentation of traditional stories and personages as part of an
affirmation of the city's stability and divine sanction. Tragic drama

was invariably accompanied by a briefer 'satyr play' to round off the event—a parodic, usually bawdy version of some aspect of, or some story related to, the main narrative.[1]

What is of most lasting importance for subsequent European literature is that not just any legendary narrative could be the subject of these dramatized narratives. Whether set in the remote mythical past (dealing, say, with a personage like Herakles or Prometheus), in the legendary history of the Trojan War and the foundation of the Greek cities, or, rather unusually, with significant events and conflicts in the recent past (Aeschylus's *Persians*, which relates events within living memory), the subject matter of tragic drama is human shipwreck of various kinds. The liturgical assembly at the Dionysia celebration is invited to contemplate disaster and suffering, chains of events unleashed by rash action and engulfing guilty and innocent alike; and this happens in the context of a celebration both of the city's solid identity and of the god associated with the dangerous realm of excess, the archetypal stranger who in some stories challenges and disrupts the city, who is the patron of non-citizens and who is also a major guarantor of the city's well-being.[2] It looks as though one of the foundational themes in this kind of celebration is *danger*: the city demonstrates its divinely anchored security by enacting various kinds of excess, invoking the divine stranger as patron, licensing excess in sexual symbol and action, reciting the narratives of 'excessive', disproportionate calamity as both warning and reassurance. Thus the narrative that will be appropriate for such an event will be one in which the effects of human choice or action are unusually far-reaching or extreme in the damage they inflict. There may be many reasons for this extremity of damage—ignorance, divine anger woven into the human story, vengeful intensity; but the point is the extremity, the sort of intensity of pain or despair that prompts speakers to say that it is better not to have been born.[3] This is highly likely to involve the death of a protagonist and several others, but it is not vital: there are instances where no-one dies, but the situation is still evidently extreme (the *Philoctetes* of Sophocles is the best example here). And it is no accident that two of the most familiar and frequently re-worked story cycles—the *Oresteia*, dealing with the fallout from the Trojan War, and the Theban legends woven around Oedipus and his family—allow a dramatization of how and why cities are founded and of the difference between functional and non-functional cities. The city exists because the spiralling of destructive vengeance has to be contained. There can be no indefinitely extended pattern of violence and counter-violence. Not all scores can be definitively settled and something else has to come into play. Cities that fail to achieve this containment are profoundly at risk (so a violent and unstable Thebes can be implicitly contrasted by Sophocles with a law-governed and problem-solving Athens[4]). Yet it is essential that the city does not forget that it exists precisely because of the ever-present risk of reversion to spirals of violence; and so it ritually recalls the injustice—or indeed the 'excessive justice' of limitless vendetta—and the frighteningly disproportionate outworkings of error and crime as the dangers which make the city necessary.

So the first point defining what makes a narrative 'tragic' in the Greek context is that it must be a narrative of risk or danger and disproportionate harm—often a danger created and intensified by agents not knowing how serious the effects of their actions will be (we shall be coming back to the theme of ignorance later on). But it must also be a narrative that is *familiar*. The challenge of the Dionysia contests is not to produce an original story but to offer a fresh reading or performance of something that is part of a shared frame of reference. The multiplication of speakers in tragic performance that was apparently the greatest change associated with Aeschylus's generation allows for diverse perspectives, and this becomes one of the main motors of what we might call properly *dramatic* development. As Aristotle will later insist, one of the distinctive things about tragedy as a discipline of composition is that it does not simply recite stories but *enacts* them[5]—and thus entails the tension of diverse voices taking the narrative forward on the basis of a range of limited views, rather than through a single definitive narrator. It is a familiar story; but its characters will have to speak from a position of not-knowing. None of them will have privileged access to the whole story. So the *event* of tragic drama comes to involve different kinds of tension—between characters in the dramatic exchange who have varying perspectives on what is happening and varying degrees of knowledge, and between an audience that knows the story and a cast of characters who don't. The performance of the narrative will be in some measure a process of discovery for the persons represented on the stage; but the discovery experienced by the audience will be something else—not a matter of finding out what is happening and will happen, but finding out some new connection between the story and the current life of the city.[6]

The tragic narrative is thus a *familiar* story about dangerous *unpredictabilities*; and there is already an obvious irony here. A repeated story may seem like one that carries no continuing threat or risk; we know the unknowns, as it were. But the fact of repetition itself declares that we have not yet—*never* yet—grasped the nature of the danger being represented. We tell the familiar story because we know that we do not yet know it. We can neither settle down either with the simple curiosity with which we encounter a new story, nor give ourselves over to a plain ritual repetition. The nature of the ritual repetition itself invites the unsettlement that will make the difference. The story is one of danger encountered and at some level survived; but if the nature of that danger is opened up for fresh representation, it is as if the surviving of it is still something of an open question: we have been reminded that we don't know yet what the scale of the danger is. So part of what's going on in the development of *tragic* narration out of the simple recitation of a narrative is that the circumstances and decisions described in the narrative are shown to be 'readable' in more than one way: and the not-knowing of the characters becomes a disturbing reflection of our own not-knowing as observers. As the dramatic complexity increases, so does the danger experienced by the audience, despite the familiarity of the story being represented. Wai Chee Dimock, in a brilliant essay which focuses on Euripides' handling of Homeric themes, notes how the role of the Chorus in these plays has become different from the way the Chorus is deployed in Aeschylus or Sophocles. While the earlier dramatists use the Chorus as a voice largely distanced from the interactions of the main speakers (granted all the qualifications that need to be made to such a statement), Euripides' Chorus is involved as the protagonists are: there is a 'breakdown of immunity', so that the choric voice speaks from *inside* the catastrophe that has overtaken the women of Troy.[7] And if the Chorus's immunity has been broken open, so has the audience's; the damage represented in the tragic narrative is not contained by any structural feature such as choric observation. And if the argument so far is correct, Euripides is really doing no more than taking forward something that is already implicit in the very fact of dramatizing the narrative, representing the familiar story through plural voices and imagined interaction.

Dimock notes that there has been much debate about the significance of the Chorus even in earlier tragedy, with the important point being made that the Chorus speaks in a formalized, archaic language clearly distinct from the idiom of the main speakers, and is also composed of figures who are not 'standard' participants in civic life—women, slaves, the elderly. One way of interpreting this is that the Chorus as such stands for the disturbing uncontainability of the effects of the actions being represented: this is not simply a story about risk to the city as collectivity but a story about the threat to 'the human voice' itself figured in the catastrophe depicted. As Dimock puts it,[8] the Chorus 'has nothing different to tell us'; it does not simply speak for a reconciled civic identity, a normative perspective completely free from the agonized conflict of the narrative itself. When Hecuba cries that 'the world is blotted out', the Chorus responds, 'All has vanished, and Troy is nothing.'[9] The Chorus is there in order to reinforce the sense of danger, to broaden the scope of the action represented and its effects. Because it stands on the edge of the action and also on the edge of the civic world (bearing in mind that Dionysos is traditionally associated with those outside the body of citizens), the Chorus, even when offering comments and drawing morals, is there to represent the porous frontier between the familiar action narrated and the assembly now gathered. It permits danger to leak into the audience.

Of course this is not an uncontrolled danger: the entire action is, as we have repeatedly noted 'liturgical', it has a ritually determined beginning and end, and the gap between audience and officiants ('performers' is the wrong word, because it implies a particular kind of gap between those enacting the drama and those simply watching) is physically marked. But the increasingly distinctive sign of tragic performance, if we are allowed to see a trajectory running from Aeschylus to Euripides, seems to be in the direction of intensifying the felt risk of the act of representation. The figures we see on the stage before us are caught up in more complex constraints than they know; every new representation adds a dimension to them, a fresh aspect of risk. The choric accompaniment to the action shows both a collective registering of the damage involved in the primary action and, increasingly, a collective contamination by that action, evidenced in the

Chorus's lack of authoritative perspective and (certainly in the *Trojan Women* of Euripides) their helpless solidarity in the sufferings of the main speakers. There is no safe place and there are no complete accounts of what the danger is and where it comes from. It may well be that Aristotle's qualms about Euripides as a dramatist (although he regards him as the 'most tragic' of the great dramatists because he does not shrink from unconsoled endings) have to do with this.[10] A Chorus that has no independent vantage point over against the main action of the drama might suggest that the playwright is overstepping certain limits, allowing what we have called a 'leakage' of danger and uncertainty into the audience so that the boundaries of the liturgical framework are pushed almost to destruction. But—to repeat a point made already—Euripides is in this respect only taking a bit further what is implicit in the whole enterprise of dramatically representing familiar stories of catastrophe. The genre as it develops *invites* just such a testing of boundaries: can the civic identity as figured in the liturgical assembly cope with this level of indeterminacy and unknown risk? If this is indeed the celebration of Dionysos, the dangerous god of excess or transgression (and so of those who are outside the city and its securities), can the liturgy ultimately contain his excessiveness in its words and rites? The extremity represented in Euripides' *Bacchae* is the most stark enactment of the risks of underrating the disruptive effect of Dionysos's presence. The continuing *practice* of liturgical tragedy assumes that it can in some degree manage, if not exactly control the Dionysian; but if we are continually faced with the challenge of handling unknown danger, danger which we are only beginning to see as such, the capacity of the liturgy to manage it has to be rediscovered again and again by posing new challenges to it, testing it to destruction.

That is one way of understanding a progression from ritual recitation to ritual enactment. The more this enactment works through diverse voices and the deployment of an ensemble of flawed and partial perspectives in those voices (including the choric voice), the more the underlying issue of articulating and coping with danger is made vivid to the audience—as a corporate and an individual question. The drama presents a double risk. The unsettling of the perspective from which we are invited to view the danger of the narrative means that we cannot be certain that it is past: what if we have not yet seen the aspect that really matters, that *really* threatens? And this entails also a danger to each individual witnessing the narrative: like the speakers on stage, I may not know what I am doing and so I may already be involved in processes over which I have no control. As an individual speaker/agent myself, I am no different from the figures represented— except in knowing their story as far as it goes. In both respects, the audience, collectively and individually, is faced with unfinished business. And the tragic imagination is defined here not as a despairing vision of the cosmos or even a convention of contemplating the disasters that overtake great and powerful figures, but as that particular kind of imagining that *stays with* the risk of returning to familiar and apparently resolved narratives of suffering and pacification and asking them new questions by finding new voices in which to tell or, better, realize the stories.

In other words, 'the tragic' is originally a function of how a verbal and visual representation works in the mind of a community gathered to celebrate or affirm its resilience and legitimacy in full awareness of the fragility that always pervades its life. It exists in the disturbing gap between that affirmation and a complementary recognition: the acknowledgement that we do not have a *final* point of view about the crises or catastrophes which both haunt and justify the existence of the political order. It would be facile to say that tragedy is thus intrinsically revolutionary (as facile as saying that it is inherently conservative, again a point to which we shall be returning); but it is a conscious testing of the strength of a settlement, and an invitation to test further, once we have recognized that every voice we encounter in the drama is provisional. As Simon Goldhill observes,[11] tragedy's effect is to 'make difficult the assumptions of the values of the civic discourse' as part of the interplay between order and excess that characterizes the Dionysia. Affirming divine sanction for the city's existence becomes something more and more hard-won as tragedy develops, even while the context and rationale remain incontestably the liturgical celebration. Take the drama out of its liturgical setting and the pressing question becomes whether there can be any corporate social identity at all: what we are left with is a stand-off between the narration of uncontainable catastrophe and the sheer convention of social identity. Holding on to the possibility of seeing tragic performance as a sort of liturgy, an ordered affirmation of community, means holding on to the belief that what we have to say to each other and what it is possible to do with and for each other in civic, law-governed community is not an arbitrary or contingent matter, a useful fiction. It has something to do with the breaking-in of energy beyond the resources of the world as we know it, the energy of the divine, however it is understood. The cohesion of the community is not simply worked out on the ground but has in it some element of 'gift', something not planned or earned. To represent pain and disaster in this public way is to call for public recognition of why such a gift matters, because of the seriousness of what happens when it is absent. So Dionysos is manifest as the power that simultaneously allows and contains excess—endorsing his divine kinswoman Athene's verdict which halts the cycle of revenge in the *Oresteia*. Excess comes to mean an excess of mercy over retribution, a declaration that the repetition of violence is not a necessity, not a law of nature. Take this away and law gives way to the endless sameness of violence; the dangerous enactment of a story by diverse voices is part of a pedagogy which leads us to see discernment and differentiation as possible, and so to *think* about what is other or strange—rather than simply to define the self (corporate or individual) against it.

II

These are large claims for classical tragedy, and they need a good deal of further refinement in relation to later versions of the genre. But if it is true that Greek tragedy deals with familiar stories in unfamiliar ways as part of a major civic event, something like this must be part of what is going on. And—as Martha Nussbaum's deservedly admired book on Greek philosophy and tragedy sets out at length[12]—the further implication is that tragedy obliges us to pay attention to sheer *circumstance*, to the different pressures and impulses that are at work on actual agents in the world; it warns us against the fantasy of a virtue that has no cost. Nussbaum's book begins with an analysis of Aeschylus's *Agamemnon* (which depicts the sacrifice of Agamemnon's daughter Iphigenia in order to placate the goddess Artemis, who is delaying the sailing of the Greek fleet to Troy).[13] The war on Troy has been commanded by Zeus and so must be pursued; it can only be pursued if the king kills his daughter. Human atrocity has to be weighed against disobedience to the supreme god, and Agamemnon

resolves to be obedient. There is thus no good option available that
does not carry with it a burden of further guilt. But what the tragedy
does, by way of the Chorus's commentary, is to question the way in
which Agamemnon performs what he decides is his duty: he sacrifices
Iphigenia without apparent regret, he 'adopts' the ill-luck of his
dilemma and presents the killing as simply a holy act. In other words,
he denies that there is a real conflict here, and he does so by refusing
to 'see what the Chorus sees'.[14] The difficulty posed by the sheer particular humanity of his daughter is swept aside; but so, in a significant
sense, is Agamemnon's own humanity. What makes him who he is at
this juncture is precisely the coincidence of competing duties, his bad
luck, to put it in the simplest terms. To deny that bad luck or to co-operate willingly with the cruel necessity that presses on him is for him
to deny the diversity of obligation that defines him, to deny that he is
enmeshed in familial duty as well as devotion to the gods. His 'virtue'
in doing what has to be done to appease Artemis and fulfil the command of Zeus is a one-dimensional thing.

It is not the purpose of the play—or of tragedy in general, it might
be argued—to tell us what a 'good' act or stance might be in such a
situation, a good act that would not be one-dimensional and untruthful.
The drama is not there to give instruction but to cast light on a set of
actions that will have catastrophic consequences. Agamemnon's killing of Iphigenia is the root of the cycle of hurt and vengeance that the
Oresteia unfolds, with more and more such conflicts of duty; but it is
not only the act of killing that poisons the moral circulatory system. It
is also the untruthfulness of Agamemnon's pretence that what he does
is holy without qualification. So that if we think of tragedy in terms of
the representation and management of danger, the danger it deals
with is not just the possibility of conflicting duties but the risk of denying the reality of the conflict and so forfeiting truthfulness, even identity. Agamemnon has lost his moral substance, silenced or killed
something of himself long before he is butchered by his wife and her
lover. In his passion to be 'good' without cost or shadow he has guaranteed that he cannot now be good at all. And, putting this together
with the point made earlier about tragedy as part of a pedagogy
equipping us to deal with difference, to think about difference, we
could say that Agamemnon's problem is that he stops *thinking*.[15] His
representation of himself becomes a willed fantasy, a deliberate

construct; in plain terms, he no longer has to worry about who he is or what he should do. He is not a stranger to himself; and one aspect of the tragic imagination is that we are made to see how strange we are to ourselves, how much in us there is to question or to be baffled by. If there is a positive hint here of what a truthfully good life might entail, Nussbaum suggests, it is that unless we recognize the role of unchosen circumstance in our decision-making, we lose all kinds of other goods: 'If we were such that we could in a crisis dissociate ourselves from one commitment because it clashed with another, we would be less good'.[16]

These are some of the ways in which tragedy in its earliest shape makes difficult both the political and the personal—or, to put it more positively, the ways in which it begins to reconstruct the political and the personal. The identity of the city is shown to be a divinely ordered balance of different obligations running in different directions and requiring law as the institutionalized means of recognizing these multiple interdependencies;[17] it is not based on a set of simple divine commands that can all be fulfilled by all agents without cost to others or attention to others. And the identity of the individual agent is accordingly represented afresh as always *implicated*: always defined by unchosen connections and the obligations that come with them. Human action is not a simple assertion of the individual will but a *thinking-through* of the diverse sorts of connection that we inhabit and the search for courses of action that are as truthful as possible and as little harmful as possible; all that within the overall recognition that there are no completely 'safe' courses, because of all that we do not and cannot know. Nussbaum pursues a similar line of reflection on the tragic in her treatment of Sophocles' *Antigone*[18]—a play that seems inexhaustible in its resonances for thinking about the tensions between personal and civic obligation, between the duty of Antigone to see that her dead brother is buried and the duty of Creon, the king, to enforce the decree he has made for the good of the city that the body of a rebel or traitor should lie unburied and unhallowed. In a well-known chorus in the play (the so-called 'Ode of Man'), we are shown various aspects of what makes human beings 'uncanny' or 'awesome' (*deinon*), including the 'passion' (*orge*) for constructing cities:[19] human beings exhibit a 'rage for order', to borrow Wallace Stevens' phrase; yet thinking about this (by definition) unbalanced impulse indicates that civic order itself is in danger of the one-dimensionality we have seen as a threat in the *Agamemnon*: 'the rage for civic control has as its other face the neglect or the harmonizing-away of the special force of each of the separate concerns that fill out the city and give it its substance'.[20] Thus the search for the reasonable and safe course of action will always bring disaster sooner or later to the extent that it presses us to ignore the unavoidable costs of safety.

But doesn't this produce a sense of paralysis in the agent, resignation to a world incapable of being tamed? This is how Schopenhauer reads tragedy, says Nussbaum, and it is closer, she thinks, to the difficult questions of the text than Hegel's better-known account, which steers us towards a more positive final position, the hope of some reconciling synthesis (we shall be coming back to Hegel's treatment of the play at more length in chapter 3).[21] What offers a way through is the appearance of the seer Tiresias towards the end of the play, after Antigone has been led off to die: he urges Creon to turn away from his rigidity and discover how to adjust his decisions to the complexity of what is before him—in other words, to learn how to act 'lawfully', in the sense we have given to this concept. And—surprisingly—the Chorus breaks in with an impassioned and memorably beautiful prayer to Dionysos to save the city: he is begged to come down in all the fire of his ecstatic excess, in his wild and erotic dancing, to save the *city*, the world of dependability, stable public reasoning. It is an affirmation, says Nussbaum,[22] of a vision of civic well-being which understands that 'justice' is bound up with acknowledged disharmony, that it is the holding of tension, not a resolving into false simplicities. As the play makes clear, there is in fact no Dionysian intervention to prevent the specific disasters that overtake Creon's family; but the concluding chorus implies that these disasters are exactly what can be expected if no attention is paid to *both* the prosaic conventions of law in the city, the pragmatic traditions of handling conflict and stress, *and* the anything but prosaic inrush of Dionysian excess, divine order (dance) in near-chaos. For Nussbaum, this hymn is not, as it is for some audiences and commentators, a piece of harshly ironic comment on the failure of the gods to speak or act, but a moment of 'healing without cure', a simple moment of acknowledging the fugitive possibility of order embodied in the very processes of turmoil or tension.

I shall have more to say later about whether Nussbaum has got Hegel's reading of the text right (not quite, I think), but the main point is a strong one: once again, the danger envisaged is a danger to law in the community and to sanity and compassion in the individual. Tragedy handles danger by challenging the idea that obligations can be so ordered that they will never collide or that the weighing of one obligation against another ends by voiding one of the competing pressures of any real force. Any aspiration to a 'just' life must incorporate a just assessment of the moral strength of alternatives (and the seriousness of the human cost involved in making a choice of one over another). And the tragic drama does this precisely by way of its distinctive innovation, the use of plural voices to represent action and so also to recreate the processes of deliberation. These voices are rhetorically sharpened so as to kindle appropriate emotion in the hearer or audience—as in the instance quoted by Nussbaum from the *Agamemnon* where the Chorus evokes the poignancy of Iphigenia's last moments, as she struggles to appeal to her father's companions and assistants, all of them well known to her from childhood, or, more starkly, in the relentless horror and pathos of both main speakers and Chorus in the *Trojan Women*.[23] Passion of a kind is thus invoked as part of moral pedagogy (a major theme of Nussbaum's book, as of her later philosophical work[24]). The *disordered* passion for simplicity or order without shadow, for control and unqualified absolution, must be undermined by the initially unlikely convergence of pragmatism and ecstasy. The ecstatic Dionysian dance holds particular passions in balance and reciprocity (otherwise there would be no *dance*); it offers an image of how each individual's specific constraints may somehow be held in a balance that is not simply a compromise. The deliberating self, always already invested or involved with strangeness (the strangeness of pressure from outside—from fate or incomprehensible divine decree—or from within, from the incomprehensible passions that are named and made visible in Dionysian ritual excess), is de-centred, dethroned, by this pedagogy—but, crucially, not deskilled or annihilated. This self is invited to a new level of attention and reflection, not with an eye to removing the diversity of pressures or duties, but so as to be able to see itself as limited yet not doomed to absolute sterility. As we shall see in more detail later on, the tragic idiom is a vehicle for managing loss by narrating it.[25] The self that can tell the story of its own loss is a self that understands and appropriates loss, suffering, failure, and other catastrophic events. These can be spoken of; we are not reduced to absolute silence or paralysis. Thus, the I that speaks on the far side of catastrophe is an I that admits both its limits and its vulnerability to damage—that presents itself as a wounded self; but in so doing declares that its reality is not dependent on success or happiness.

This, presumably, is what is implied in the often-quoted story of the Russian poet Anna Akhmatova. She stood regularly for months on end in the queues outside Stalin's jails with food parcels for her imprisoned son, along with scores of other women in the same plight. One day she was recognized; a woman asked her if she could describe the situation, and she replied, 'Yes.' 'Something like a smile crossed the woman's face.'[26] Worth and truth are not fictions so long as something can be *said*, even if the saying is not more than 'description', because description itself changes something and establishes that there remains a world in which speakers can understand one another. So the act of representing catastrophe is a testing of the resilience not only of the city's order but of the self's order (its groundedness, its 'legitimacy', its capacity to sustain itself): the narrating of suffering reminds us of the inescapability of risk wherever we look, and also of a surviving freedom to look and to speak. Failure, ignorance, and hurt can be 'exceeded'; not (to use Nussbaum's terminology) cured but in some sense healed by representation. The drama tells us that many of the choices we make are made in such ignorance (culpable or not) that their effect will be damage to us and others, out of proportion to merit or guilt; and this unsparing message is not a message that pushes us towards passivity or hopelessness simply because it is spoken in the context of a common ritual. Speaking about and showing the risk of disaster and the cost of different sorts of loss, in a language that is not just individual but allows listening and sharing of perception and emotion—this liturgical activity is way of affirming our recognition of one another as participants in a continuing labour. And it signifies that we—as a community and as individuals within it—are not exhausted by either the experience or the memory of loss.

The tragic enactment does not provide a happy ending in the sense that individual agents are rescued, healed, or even absolved. But I think we have to say—in contrast to those who want tragedy in its purest form to be essentially about what is never healed or about a fatal rupture in being itself such that human beings are unwelcome in the world[27]—that it does not insist on a purely and simply unreconciled conclusion either. The act of representing carries implications; the describing of atrocity changes things by enforcing upon us the urgency of containing its effects. And of course to make sure that this is not a covert way of softening the atrocity or making more bearable what should be terrible to us, the tragic dramatist must keep up the pressure of shock or grief. As we shall see shortly, in looking more closely at some of Euripides' texts, the narrative has to be purged of consoling aspects: if there is consolation it is in the bare fact of narration, as for Akhmatova's neighbour in the prison queue. Damage must be insisted on; and one way of reading the movement from Aeschylus to Euripides is, as Dimock suggests, as a gradual reduction of the space of 'immunity', the space for what is not touched by catastrophe. The significance of the rite of representation is intensified the more the narrative is stripped of safe places: the one 'safe place' is simply and precisely the present moment in which damage is being enacted and spoken of, the moment we as audience cannot escape but in which we are assured that the damage enacted does not silence the self or the city.

Implicit in this is a theme to which we shall be coming back. To *avoid* confronting the worst atrocity is to make the self and the city less secure; to be silent about extremes of suffering is, by a stark paradox, to invite a more serious risk of being 'silenced' as an active self or a civic community, because what we do not name or confront, what we refuse to know, becomes the greater danger. It is not a matter of what Freudians call the 'return of the repressed'—not a matter of readjusting unbalanced forces inside the self. It has to do rather with the risk we run if we make the tacit admission that there are matters that *cannot be seen or spoken*—as if Akhmatova had said 'No' in the prison queue. And this means an expanded sphere for the terror of what we do not know, and thus an expanded place for action that arises from ignorance and anxiety; we become locked more firmly into the very mechanisms from which the drama is supposed to deliver us. This is why the tragic imagination at times takes a familiar story and intensifies its horror—why Shakespeare abandoned the traditional ending of the story of King Lear (the king restored, Cordelia alive), why Euripides introduced into the already bloodstained career of Medea her murder of her own children. It is emphatically a dangerous strategy for a genre dealing with danger. It is possible to pile up the detail of atrocities or vivid representations, visual or verbal, of atrocities with no clear ritual structure to hold the present moment of paradoxical 'safety' (thus Bret Easton Ellis's brutal satire, *American Psycho*, is not tragic in any interesting sense) and so to lose the point of the dramatic representation itself—which is to allow the audience to appropriate their own danger, with intense feeling but without panic, in a shared linguistic event. The question of what imaginative boundaries are needed to contain the representation of suffering in manageable ways is not a simple one: the controversies provoked in the UK in recent years by the work of Edward Bond and Sarah Kane bring this into sharp focus. These are dramatists whose work has stirred disgust in some because of the unrelieved and extreme horrors portrayed—extreme sexual violence, the killing of children, cannibalism, and so on.[28] But this is a necessary risk (if some representations did not overstep the bounds of 'safety', there would be no genuine risk in the first place) if we are serious about the role of tragic drama in simultaneously disturbing and re-establishing a human identity, personal and social.

III

Euripides' play *Medea*, recently and very effectively revived in two notably different London productions,[29] draws together many of the main themes of tragic imagination as sketched here, and a brief look at this drama may bring them into sharper focus. It is a play about a woman who kills her children partly as an act of revenge against a husband who is deserting her. The extreme horror and pathos of Euripides' presentation of this has guaranteed that its performance history has been sporadic; the emotional challenge is enormous. But it is also a play unmistakeably about the city—about the status (or lack of it) of non-citizens, about Athens as a sanctuary, even for those who have offended most conspicuously against the moral law, about the effect of breaking family loyalties, and much else. We first meet Medea in the words of the nurse, who describes her state of desperation and near-hysteria: she has abandoned her own city and family for Jason, but their union is not officially sanctioned by the laws of the city where they now live (Corinth), and Jason is about to marry the daughter of Corinth's ruler. Medea is convinced that this will be the prelude to her own expulsion and that of her sons from the city; she will belong nowhere, because she has so violently cut her ties with her own home. She has abandoned her father and killed her brother (5.166–7).[30] She protests to the Chorus that she accepts the constraints that lie upon the resident foreigner in a city; she is not out to be a thorn in their flesh (7.223–4). But an abandoned woman cannot be expected to accept her fate without complaint or indeed revenge, even more so if she is an alien, since she is left without any community. The Chorus agrees that vengeance against Jason will be justifiable (8.277–8), and Medea's fears are shown to be well founded when Creon, the ruler of Corinth, appears and confirms that she and her children will be exiled. He refuses Medea's plea for clemency, unpersuaded that her fury against Jason will not translate into fury against himself and his family, and thus the city also. He loves his family more than Medea, and his homeland next after them—prompting Medea to lament again her alienation from both (10.327–9). Eventually, he grants her a day's grace. The Chorus echoes Medea's grief at the prospect of her impending homelessness; but Medea announces that she will use the amnesty Creon has allowed to plot the deaths of Creon, Jason, and his new wife. But she recognizes that she will need to secure some place of future refuge, which may require her to move slowly in her plotting. The Chorus deplores the city in which oaths (Jason's to Medea) can be set aside so easily and praises Medea for providing a new model for women's agency in the unjust male world: in a context where a woman can be made invisible, rendered stateless and without rights, drastic action is needed (12.410–44).

There follows a passionate debate between Medea and Jason himself, who offers various defences and rationalizations of his behaviour: he has done his best to shield Medea from exile, he says, but her own extreme reaction has sealed her fate, and the best he now can do is to make sure that she and the children will be provided for. Medea in reply reminds him of what she has done for him and the guilt she has incurred in order to keep him safe: she has 'earned the hatred of those dear to me at home' as well as many others (14.506–7). Jason is unmoved: he ascribes his rescue from the perils of his voyages to divine protection rather than Medea's actions, and it is in fact she who is the real beneficiary of their relationship, as she has been delivered from the barbarian world into the land of Greece, where law prevails

(15.534–40). But in any case, his new marriage to Creon's daughter was always meant to guarantee a secure place in Corinth for the whole family; if Medea were not blinded by sexual jealousy and frustration, she would see the common sense of all this. Her destitution is, ultimately, her own choice; but Jason will guarantee that she has an introduction to friends elsewhere who will look after her interests (17.610–14). Medea—not surprisingly—refuses help on these terms. The Chorus again underlines the terror of being city-less, a fate literally worse than death in their eyes.

At this point (18–21.758), there is a surprising episode of relief—a new voice enters the conversation, and the style shifts abruptly to the rapid exchange of single lines between the characters (*stichomythia*). Aigeus, ruler of Athens, comes on stage, returning to his city after consulting the oracle at Delphi, and hears Medea's story; she begs him for sanctuary and promises that if he will take her under his roof she will bear him the children he longs for. He makes a solemn oath to receive and protect her; and in the light of this promise Medea is now free to pursue her plot to kill her rival by giving her an enchanted or poisoned wreath and robe. She further declares that she now intends also to kill her children, as the most effective way to injure Jason. The Chorus draws back, reminding her (23–4.865) that such an action is outside the law, but she is adamant, and proceeds to tell Jason that she has seen reason; she will accept exile without protest and leave her children with their father. She asks permission to present Jason's new bride with a robe and crown, and sends the children to petition Creon's daughter to allow them to stay, and to present Medea's gifts in person.

A long soliloquy (28–9.1081) presents Medea's vacillations (there is some scholarly debate as to whether all of this is original): she has now in fact secured 'a city and a home' for the children; but she cannot bear the thought either that they will be insulted or injured by her enemies and rivals, or that she herself will be made a fool of because she has accepted defeat. The Chorus reflects on the torments of anxiety that go with parenthood; then the news arrives that Medea's plan has been successful. Creon and his daughter have died in agony, unsparingly described by the Messenger who enters to tell Medea she must flee at once. She welcomes the news and repeats her resolve to kill the children. Despite the Chorus's invocation to the gods to prevent this, their hymn is interrupted by the screams for help of the children off-stage. When Jason enters in search of Medea, the Chorus tells him to prepare for a worse horror than he has yet seen; Medea appears in semi-divine splendour, mounted in the dragon-chariot inherited from her ancestor, the Sun-god, and, in a further impassioned dialogue, with sections of intensely worded *stichomythia*, she lays the blame for everything on Jason's arrogance and folly. She promises that in Athens she will bury her children and establish a ritual commemoration of her crimes, then curses Jason, predicting his death. She repeats with startling directness that she has killed the children to cause him pain (38.1398), and leaves him distraught. The final, very brief chorus is the stock ending to many Euripidean tragedies, simply stating that 'the god has found a way to accomplish the unexpected' (38.1419).

It is a narrative of nightmare intensity, and the figure of Medea continues to provoke all sorts of questions—not least because at the end she appears not only as protected by the gods but in something like divine form. The interweaving of fundamental tragic themes is very dense indeed. Medea has been brought in from outside, a barbarian who has become partly naturalized in the city, where, as Jason complacently announces, law and reason prevail (15.534–40).[31] But the city—through its ruling authority—proves to be unjust and unreasonable; Creon colludes with Jason's oath-breaking and is now proposing to expel Medea, offering no justification but his own decision. This is a city whose 'reason' has broken down, just as the personal fidelity of a marriage has broken down. How is it now possible to *live* in the absence of the assumption of linguistic security that is represented by civic (publicly explainable or defensible) justice and marital promise-keeping? Medea's answer is to insist on 'excessive justice', the quasi-law of vengeance. Suffering has been caused and must be caused in return, and the rationale of appropriate action becomes the causing of maximal pain. In other words, the most serious danger being represented here is the danger of the dissolution of law itself in favour of the repetition of violence; the traditional resolution of tragic conflict, as in the *Oresteia*, is denied. But the Medea who—so to speak—breaks through to the ultimate point of repetitive violence in her horrific killings is also the figure who will now move on to be part of the foundation of another city. Athens has promised her refuge, and to Athens she will go, to bear children for Aigeus—to secure a future for lawful rule in the city—and to create a liturgy that commemorates her own excess in vengeance. It is as though, having exhausted the possibilities of lawlessness, Medea has the freedom as no-one else does to see why the city and its rituals must be reinvented when the city's justice collapses, not replaced by vendetta and fragmentation. All the way through the play we are reminded again and again that being city-less is the worst thing that can happen: Medea's often confused and contradictory rationalizations of her own behaviour have one absolutely consistent theme, the terror, for herself and her children, of being outside civic peace and security. She has sacrificed her own partial peace and security, her ancestral loyalties (even though Jason seems not to recognize the seriousness of her breach with her kindred, since she is a 'barbarian' and thus deemed incapable of such loyalty[32]), and is now faced with a future in which neither ancestral belonging nor law-governed reciprocity can give her a guaranteed identity. She is desperate for the civic peace whose vestiges she so horrendously rips apart by her murders.

So the audience of *Medea* is faced with a story about what happens to a city that forgets its duty to the solemn compacts between persons and allows these to be overridden by expediency and the desire for prosperity; and what happens is that appalling actions arise in the absence of social trust and equity. Only in facing the possible terrors of this situation can the audience grasp why the law of the city matters as it does; and they learn this through the narrative of an outsider who knows better than anyone what it is to be 'city-less'—both a barbarian and a criminal, as well as being a woman, whose belonging in the community is always dependent on a male partner's standing. But in addition to this, we have to consider the shocking implication of the final scenes of the drama. The Chorus invokes the divine powers of earth and sun to prevent the slaughter of the children; but if there is an answer to this prayer, it is the epiphany of Medea in the heavens, riding in the chariot of the sun. The power of the earth and sun to mend the broken bonds of the city is manifest in the glorified transgressor: the mending power is only released when the worst has happened and been named and embodied. Jason has earlier tried to make light of Medea's part in saving him from danger and prefers to ascribe this to a conventional pattern of divine grace: it was *really* Aphrodite who did it all (15.528), a nicely ironic inversion of the scepticism that would prefer to see human agency at work in events rather than divine. But at the end of the play, his interpretation of events is brutally overturned: not only has no divine protector stepped in to spare him the horror of his children's deaths; his apparently human protector has turned out to be a semi-divine enemy. His betrayal of the bonds that civic solidarity is meant to preserve is avenged by an unsuspected 'deity', Medea, terrifyingly transfigured, who proceeds to re-establish civic piety in Athens. She has become a spectacular example of that dual identity, saviour and outcast, which recurs so frequently in discussions of the sacred, the *pharmakon* that is both poison and cure. Interestingly, Aristotle[33] clearly disliked this denouement as introducing directly into the action the kind of supernatural get-out-of-jail card that ought to be resolutely avoided *within* the dramatic action. But it is exactly this bold solecism in Euripides' text that obliges us to look harder to see what point is being driven home; and there is a strong case for seeing it as a deliberate reinforcement of one of the fundamental themes of tragedy as such.

As in the *Oresteia* and in Sophocles' Theban plays, Athens is portrayed as the archetypal city in which tragic catastrophe is somehow contained and the cycle of violence and revenge arrested; but Euripides, with his usual edginess, leaves us with a supernaturally transfigured benefactress of Athens who is also the representative of several different kinds of rejected and marginal existence and who embodies danger, the threat to the city, in an unusually extreme way, as a violator of both family and civic solidarity. It is difficult to know exactly what Euripides is doing in painting this heavily shadowed picture; but one credible way of reading it is that he is implicitly telling his audience that unexamined solidarity (whether it is the life of Medea's 'barbarian' kindred or the complacent self-serving of Creon and Jason) has to be broken down before a genuinely 'lawful', self-reflective civic identity can be secured. Athens is not simply the archetypal city but the archetypal *self-aware* city. A primordial community solidarity which refuses to face the power of the extreme (including the power of sexual passion, of which Jason so rashly makes light in his first argument with Medea) and so does not understand the depth of risk in human affairs, is painfully fragile. Imagine this solidarity disrupted in the most violent ways possible, and you will have made some advance towards a justice that takes into account the complex diversity of actual human interaction. This takes us back to Martha Nussbaum's analysis, and her proposal that a serious and defensible account of human goodness will confirm the positive value of its 'fragility'—in the sense that the attentiveness, empathic intelligence, and imagination that comes from recognizing the constraints under which we all act enhance the texture and depth of our moral life. And it is in the tragic imagination's calling-up for us the seemingly uncontrollable pain of disruption that we begin to learn how we might face danger without denial and make some sense of the aspiration towards a humanly and flexibly just order, towards law, towards an imagined 'Athens'.

IV

One implication of this, which we shall be exploring at greater length later on, is that the relation of tragedy with conflicting imperatives is more complicated than might at first appear. In nineteenth- and twentieth-century discussion, we have become so used to seeing Sophocles' *Antigone* as somehow the definitive tragic narrative that we ignore other structural pressures in the tragic drama of Athens.[34] *Medea* makes little sense in terms of clashing imperatives; likewise *Trojan Women*. As Kevin Wetmore observes in a notable study of African-American appropriations of Greek tragedy,[35] the Medea story was used to 'frame' the case of Margaret Garner, a nineteenth-century African-American slave who killed her small daughter to prevent the child being returned to slavery. A well-known painting by Thomas Satterwhite Noble was entitled *Margaret Garner, or the Modern Medea*; and the event furnished the core of Toni Morrison's novel, *Beloved*. But this use of the Medea typology is in fact deeply problematic: the tragic choice made by Margaret Garner is between the good of life and the good of freedom for her child, and what made the event shocking—in a salutary way—for nineteenth-century North America was precisely the assumption that life in slavery was so appalling a prospect that death was preferable. In other words, it is an *Antigone*-style choice between real rival goods, in a way that is by no means the clear or dominant theme of Euripides' play. His Medea does indeed repeatedly invoke the fear of life in exile, outside any civic community, for herself and her sons. Yet the motivations she articulates are bewilderingly diverse and inconsistent; they involve at some points her own honour, at others the urge to inflict the greatest hurt. The idea that she is acting to spare her children suffering surfaces at one or two moments, but to treat this as her chief concern is to sentimentalize the story. Noble's picture attempts to cast an 'ennobling' classical light on Margaret Garner's action, but at the price both of softening and simplifying the contours of the Medea story and of blurring the terrible specificity of Margaret Garner's dilemma.

The tragic collision of duties or imperatives is—in the context of what has been outlined so far—*one* of the constraints that may push us towards disproportionately damaging action, but not necessarily the most significant one. To treat it as the only one that matters is a step towards the not very helpful modern argument as to whether and in what sense tragedy demands a central figure who is distinguished by 'nobility' of spirit, a figure who is morally sophisticated enough to grasp the seriousness of rival imperatives. But tragedy does not affect only the morally sophisticated. Aristotle indeed saw tragedy as a narrative about 'better than average'—fundamentally right-minded but not heroically virtuous—people pushed into disastrous and destructive actions; but this is not the same as ascribing to them a kind of extra charism, realized in the way they handle their profound inner conflicts. The underlying thing, which makes tragic narrative what it is, is that personal and social orders are exposed as breakable, and, more specifically, exposed as endangered by a persistent refusal to look truthfully at their opposites—at the collapse of reasoned action and acceptable, coherent images of the self in the face of vengeful or jealous passion, at the collapse of civic order in the face of vendetta or corruption. Too much stress on tragic inner conflict makes the genre more individualistic or apolitical than it really is—and Aristotle, with his clear focus on the structures and processes of *composition* in tragedy rather than the initial context of liturgical performance, is already pointing in this general direction. Hence the insistence in this chapter on the interweaving of civic and personal crisis in the early texts. We miss something essential if we fail to see the tragic imagination as a political imagination; if it works as it does to reshape a sense of selfhood, that is largely because of the inseparability between personal and civic that characterizes the sensibility of the Greek world.

'It is possible to mean well, to be caring and kind, loving one's neighbour as oneself, yet to be complicit in the corruption and violence

of social institutions. Furthermore, this predicament may not corre-
spond to, and may not be represented by, *any available politics or knowledge.*'[36] This is Gillian Rose's observation on the risks we run in trying
to construct edifying representations of atrocity, specifically in connection with what is or can or should be 'represented' at the site of
the Auschwitz camps. Her—difficult—point is that, insofar as we
can think of appropriate representation, it must avoid creating an
(essentially passive) sense of solidarity, or even self-questioning ('Could
I have done this?'). For her, these are edifying strategies, and thus
inimical to both the tragic and the politically transformative. If there
can be fitting representation, its aim is to raise the issue of what has
happened to *institutions* that permit or enable atrocity—and thus of
what has happened to our sense of ourselves as moral agents in
public relationships. Linking this with our discussion so far, we could
say that Rose is implicitly inviting the work of a tragic imagination
in which we are obliged to confront the vulnerability of institutions in
direct connection with the vulnerability of our self-images; and this is
indeed what the earliest tragedies propose. The horror of the Shoah is
partly the horror of extreme evil motivation and action, the tearing-up
of social bonds; but it is also a narrative of people who failed to recognize their capacity as political agents and colluded with the normaliza-
tion of tyranny and mass murder, the eradication of true political life.
A tragic representation thus shows not only the fact of atrocity—
though it has to face this and decide how it is dramatically shown; it
must also show an audience the seriousness of the danger they daily
face in their political life. It must restore the passion for law and over-
turn the passion for 'order' in the crude (fascist) sense. And so it must
also tell us again what we do not know and cannot know, warning us
against claims to final orderliness and reasonableness, reconnecting
us with whatever possibility we still possess of building the sacred into
our politics. We acknowledge that human agents deserve and require
unconditional and particularized attention, need to be *imagined* in all
their diversity and confusion, because only this will break through into
the radical patience of law, taking the time needed to do justice.

Aristotle identified two key moments in tragic drama, 'reversal' and
'recognition' (*peripeteia* and *anagnorisis*).[37] Tragedy must deal with very
visible and eventful change from better to worse, with the destruction

of institutions and persons. And it must allow for the coming to light of what has been hidden, both for good and for ill. Sometimes (ideally, for Aristotle, which is why he sees the Theban cycle as something of a paradigm), the coming to light is what brings about the reversal of fortune. The two moments are clearly recognizable in Gillian Rose's comments. Tragic representation confronts the imagination with pictures of utterly unpredictable dissolutions of social solidarity and humanist stability; it uncovers not so much the unknown as the *fact* of our not-knowing. When, in accord with the assumptions of classical Greek drama, it deals with a story we already know—and the narrative of Auschwitz is a story we undeniably know—its task is to persuade us that at some significant level we have *never* really known it; that there is no finished narration but only the continuing exposure of ourselves to ever-new perspectives on the danger concealed in where and who we think we are. Yet this constantly changing and expanding representation of danger seeks to move us towards truthful and just action in the city; it does not offer any consolation about the past but, by the plain act of liturgical showing-forth, tells us that disaster can be shown in a way that changes the world we inhabit. And to think of it in terms of liturgy connects it with more overtly religious language about 'conversion', in the biblical sense of a radical change of perception. It is a reminder of why a dramatic representation that shows us what disaster does not silence or exhaust might be called a showing of the sacred, that excess of unearned, unexpected life that sustains us in going on speaking and thinking.

Notes

1. For a good basic discussion of Greek tragedy, see Jennifer Wallace, *The Cambridge Introduction to Tragedy*, Cambridge University Press 2007, pp.10–30; in more detail, Simon Goldhill, *Reading Greek Tragedy*, Cambridge University Press 1986 and *Sophocles and the Language of Tragedy*, Oxford University Press 2012.
2. On Dionysos, see especially Richard Seaford, *Dionysos*, London, Routledge 2006 (chapter 7 on theatre and pp.27–30 on the involvement of slaves in Dionsyian celebrations). A more idiosyncratic study is *Dionysos* by Maria Daraki, Paris, Arthaud 1985, particularly chapter 3. J. Winkler and F. Zeitlin (eds), *Nothing to Do With Dionysus? Athenian Drama in its Social Context*, Princeton University Press 1989, is an important collection of essays on the increasing complexity of Athenian tragedy and its drift away from strictly liturgical roots.

3. 'Not to be born is best'; from *Oedipus at Colonus* as translated by Robert Fagles, *Sophocles: The Three Theban Plays*, Harmondsworth, Penguin Classics 1984 (revised), p.358, l.1388. Future references to the Theban plays will be to this translation, by page and line number.

4. This is very noticeable in *Oedipus at Colonus*; Oliver Taplin, in the introduction to his excellent new translation of the play (*Sophocles: Four Tragedies*, Oxford University Press 2015, pp.217–19), outlines the argument, but cautions against reading this to mean that Thebes is intrinsically evil rather than a 'failed state' which could be restored to functional life.

5. Aristotle, *Poetics*, translated by John Warrington, London, Dent (Everyman's Library) 1963, 1449b, III.A, p.12.

6. Euripides' *Trojan Women* is commonly thought to be a response to the contemporary Athenian devastation of the island of Melos in 415 BCE, during the Peloponnesian War.

7. Wai Chee Dimock, 'After Troy: Homer, Euripides, Total War', in Rita Felski (ed.), *Rethinking Tragedy*, Baltimore MD, Johns Hopkins University Press 2008, pp.66–81; quotation from p.78.

8. Ibid.

9. Ibid., p.79, quoting from Philip Vellacott's translation, *Euripides: The Women of Troy*, Harmondsworth, Penguin Classics 1965, p.123.

10. Aristotle, *Poetics*, tr Warrington, 1453a, p.22.

11. Simon Goldhill, 'The Great Dionysia and Civic Ideology', *Journal of Hellenic Studies* 107 (1987), p.74.

12. Martha Nussbaum, *The Fragility of Goodness: Luck and Ethics in Greek Tragedy and Philosophy*, Cambridge University Press 1986.

13. Ibid., pp.32–50.

14. Ibid., p.36.

15. Ibid., pp.42–3.

16. Ibid., p.50.

17. Cf. Gillian Rose, *Mourning Becomes the Law: Philosophy and Representation*, Cambridge University Press 1996, p.75: 'The law is the falling towards or away from mutual recognition, the triune relationship, the middle, formed or deformed by reciprocal self-relations.'

18. Nussbaum, *The Fragility of Goodness*, chapter 3.

19. Tr. Fagles, pp.76–7.

20. Nussbaum, *The Fragility of Goodness*, p.75.

21. Ibid., p.79.

22. Ibid., p.82.

23. As noted earlier, the Chorus here is echoing rather than challenging or commenting upon what is said by the main speakers.

24. See, for example, Martha Nussbaum, *Upheavals of Thought: The Intelligence of Emotions*, Cambridge University Press 2001.

25. Gillian Rose writes of 'inaugurated mourning', a sort of intelligent grieving which makes a difference to how we think about trauma without offering a happy outcome; see pp.145–8 below.

26. The story is told 'Instead of a Preface' to Akhmatova's long poem of 1957, 'Requiem'. The poem is translated by Avril Pyman, *Requiem*, Durham, Black Cygnet Press 2002.

27. See chapter 4 on the idea of 'absolute tragedy'.

28. See chapter 4 for a longer discussion of Sarah Kane's work.

29. At the National Theatre in 2014, directed by Carrie Cracknell, and at the Almeida in 2015 (in Rachel Cusk's adaptation), directed by Rupert Goold.

30. Page and line references are to the translation by James Morwood in Oxford World's Classics, *Euripides: Medea and Other Plays*, Oxford University Press 1997.

31. The force of this is already weakened, since Jason has earlier (13.447–9) rebuked Medea for not giving way to 'people who are stronger than you'.

32. This is the implication of the exchanges in their first conversation, pp.13–17.

33. *Poetics*, tr. Warrington, 1454b, p.27.

34. On *Antigone* and its transformations, see chapter 3 below; and cf. George Steiner, *Antigones*, Oxford University Press 1984, for a pyrotechnically speculative if not always persuasive set of reflections on these transformations.

35. Kevin Wetmore, *Black Dionysus: Greek Tragedy and African American Theatre*, Jefferson NC, McFarland 2003.

36. Gillian Rose, *Judaism and Modernity: Philosophical Essays*, Oxford, Blackwell 1993, p.35 (italics in original).

37. *Poetics*, tr. Warrington, 1452a–1452b, pp.19–21.

2

Acknowledgement and Hiddenness

What Does Tragedy Make us Know?

I

The notion of a 'danger concealed in where and who we think we are' is at the most obvious level a matter of learning to regard ourselves as opaque to ourselves: we do not yet know and shall in fact never know what we may be capable of, what pressures act upon us, what compulsions subconsciously shape our negotiation with the world. We do not own our history any more than we own our future, in the sense of having it at our disposal. St Augustine's famous discussion of memory in his *Confessions* is perhaps the first point in European intellectual history where we find a recognition of our inaccessibility to ourselves. What he calls 'the broad plains and caves and caverns of memory'[1] contain territories to which we have no easy or rapid access: 'I myself cannot grasp the totality of what I am.'[2] And if we are inaccessible to ourselves, if we cannot fully grasp or survey the content of our own subjectivity, any order we imagine in our lives is going to have a fragile quality to it. The tragic imagination, then, insists that we remain alert to the possibility that we are already incubating seeds of destruction; that our habitual discourse with ourselves as well as with others may already have set us on a path that will consume us. Tragic representation displays this and so is inevitably a paradoxical discourse—what is said is true, but also true in a sense that will disturb the frame of reference it starts from. Tragedy represents that dangerous element in our language which allows it to loosen its tie with what we think is straightforward perception. Oedipus at the beginning of *Oedipus the King* delivers a long address to the Chorus which is packed with ironies. The Thebans have prayed to the gods: Oedipus will respond to their prayers and provide the healing they beg for by uncovering the hidden guilt that has doomed the city. He pronounces a curse on the murderer of King Laius—a curse even on himself should he prove to be inadvertently harbouring the criminal—and condemns the guilty person to go forever without the shelter of the city. As Laius's successor, Oedipus has, he announces, given the dead king the offspring he never had: 'our seed might be the same' (173.296–7).[3] Oedipus will avenge him as if he were his own son. And so, with almost every line of this lengthy speech, Oedipus in his ignorance predicts and invites his own fate. What he does not know will kill him. And we as an audience are not *delivered* from our ignorance about ourselves by this, but we are warned against ignoring it. Our understanding of our neighbours is enhanced as we recognize the danger we share in our ignorance: the city is there to give us the structures we need to *admit* ignorance of ourselves and each other, and to provide an identity that we can all know, the identity of citizens under law.

So far, so clear. But there is another level at which knowledge and ignorance come into play, the level whose best expositor in contemporary reflection has been Stanley Cavell, both as critic and as philosopher.[4] Tragedy, Cavell insists, is also about what we *know* and do not acknowledge. And what we know is that we are always already involved in relation with our fellow human beings in the sheer process of self-awareness. Tragedy in this context means the failure to *acknowledge what we know* and the consequences of that. If we do not 'yield to what we know', in Cavell's formulation,[5] we are likely to be in thrall to an illusion that is both philosophically and psychologically poisonous— the fantasy that we can know ourselves and others in a way beyond the ordinary exchanges of finite speech and interaction. We seek a complete and unmediated transparency and fail to tolerate the ordinary uncertainty that attends the ordinary certainties we enjoy. Thus—to take Cavell's most extended discussion[6]—what is tragic in *Othello* is that its main character allows himself to be persuaded that what he knows is not enough: he is presented with 'evidence' for an imagined state of affairs which, although it has no confirmation beyond Iago's interpretation of a single phenomenon, offers him 'knowledge' beyond what he already has, and he proves unable to resist the offer. Othello's desire is to know everything about the woman he loves, oblivious of the fact that she is always going to be 'other' to him. 'Nothing could be more certain to Othello than that Desdemona exists; is flesh and blood; is separate from him; other'.[7] He is appalled at the thought that he would not be able to tell from her behaviour whether she had just come from another's bed, that he could have been (has been?) happy in ignorance, that he would *prefer* not to know and yet now cannot be content not to know. 'What sense had I in her stol'n hours of lust?...I had been happy if the general camp,/ Pioneers and all, had tasted her sweet body,/ So I had nothing known' (III.3). Having once allowed the possibility that there are things he did not know, could not have known, he is now greedy to know without shadow or doubt: 'Villain, be sure thou prove my love a whore' (ibid.). Like someone instantly enthralled by an addictive drug, he needs more; he needs to master this newly revealed possibility of a knowledge that penetrates beyond the routine assurances of a developing relationship. The otherness of the woman he loves tells him that he is dependent and partial—in fact, that he is *human*. That is what he is ultimately refusing, and that is what exacts tragic consequences. Denying the other (which is what is entailed in the desire for the other to be completely known) is a step towards the death of the other, but also a step towards the death of the self, the denial of the human in oneself as in the other; because the other who is denied is the self's other, invested in myself and itself equally.

The tragic imagination, then, arises in part from what Cavell calls 'a horror that proposes our lack of certain access to other minds'.[8] When such horror enters our consciousness, we embark on the obsessional and doomed project of dissolving the other's distance—by torture, perhaps, which will deliver up what is hidden to us; by literal or metaphorical espionage, seeking to catch out the other in concealment; by the withdrawal of human empathy that allows us to adopt and defend reductive accounts of the other's behaviour and motivation; ultimately by seeking the other's death. Tragic drama displays what happens when the human is denied—not in the simple sense of outrages against human dignity or right, but at the level of deeply buried and hidden anxiety about *what I already know*: what I know in the very act of knowing, because to know is to imagine myself engaged, invested, a participant in language and so in interdependence. Connecting this with Gillian Rose's formulation about what cannot be represented in 'any available politics or knowledge',[9] we could say that there is no system of thought that will guarantee us immunity from Cavell's 'horror', from the fear of yielding to the dependence we enact every time we reflect or speak or act purposefully. Othello's panic can always be kindled into life by circumstance, by malicious intervention or traumatic experience—including the experience of having our own humanity denied.

But does this connect at all with the classical model we looked at in the last chapter? Think back to the events of *Medea*: Medea is threatened with expulsion from the city and from the only kindred she has; she responds by declaring, in effect, that if she has to exist without the bonds of social affirmation, no-one else should be allowed to live within them. Her denied humanity brings a denial of human space to others. This is not, of course, the same kind of anxiety that Cavell is discussing, but there are some continuities that can be usefully drawn out. In the classical context, the city where tragedy occurs fails or refuses to know that it encompasses strangers: it finds its strength in marking out a territory that it alone will define (irrespective, as we have seen, of true lawfulness); it is indifferent to the inwardness of the stranger and to the way in which that inwardness constitutes part of its own inwardness. This is one of the ways in which the city is unstable and makes itself increasingly unstable, with the effects we know, the personal disaster and corporate pollution which tragedy displays. For a classical audience to rediscover why the law of the city matters is for it to acknowledge that this law is precisely what permits the stranger to be a citizen, what lifts human solidarity from the level of the merely local or ethnic. Once again, what makes Athens the city as it should be, as opposed to chaotic and bloodstained Thebes, is that it seeks ways of accommodating the stranger: in Sophocles' *Oedipus at Colonus*, Theseus, greeting the exiled Oedipus, declares, 'I will never shrink/ from a stranger, lost as you are now' (318.636–7), even that the presence of the accursed exile will be a blessing for Athens (324.736–7). Oedipus can become a citizen of Athens, protected by the same laws that protect all Athenians (323.722–4). But Thebes has dealt with Oedipus's polluting crime by casting him out—just as he was initially cast out as an infant by his parents; these acts of exclusion are at the root of the horrors that afflict the city.

So one aspect of what is enacted in classical tragedy is the force and consequence of denial, of the refusal of the stranger, in the name of a law and reason which have not yet come to terms with how law must learn to inscribe the stranger in its own self-definitions. Reason, the possibility of a discourse that limits violence and rivalry, implies the readiness to *work* at strangeness. Refusing this labour, so far from reinforcing, actually wounds the speaking community and its members. In this perspective, tragic representation, diagnosing and articulating the varieties of damage that communities may undergo, aims less at healing wounds than at avoiding future denial: the classical audience is supposed to be learning how to let its own partial rationality be suspended in the excess of Dionysiac liturgy so as to have its dangerously limited certainties challenged, changed, and absorbed in a more solid and 'lawful' reasoning. And in this connection, Cavell's analysis of the role in non-classical tragedy of our failure to 'yield to what we know' suggests that the Shakespearean and post-Shakespearean tragic imagination is not simply starting afresh but translating a classical concern into the terms of an era far more intensely conscious of individual agency or destiny. But this means that the 'dangerously limited certainties' in question have to do now not with distortions of the law of the city but with misconceivings of the self. As we shall see, these continue to overlap—far more than many presentations of classical and Shakespearean tragedy might lead you to think—but it is undeniable that a different strand has entered the tragic imagination with the arrival of a consciousness conscious of its own inner tension between dependence and freedom, and capable also of *refusing* to be conscious of its own urge to resolve the tension in favour of a fantasized freedom. This is imagined as a freedom not only from external involvement, the 'investment' of self and other, but also as a freedom to encompass, control, and ultimately 'de-realize' the other. Tragedy, then, is not simply a matter of the community's failure to know what law is, but of an individual's refusal of law—of what Gillian Rose calls the 'full mutual recognition' which is law, ethical life, *Geist*.[10] The tragic becomes a catastrophic failure of recognition: I cannot recognize in the distance of the other a self-relatedness inseparable from and parallel to my own. In the simplest terms, the other whom I encounter is someone who is there for herself as I am for myself—but also someone for whom *I* am there as she is for me, someone whose self-definition and even self-awareness includes me as mine includes her. But this is a difficult recognition, and it is easier for the other to remain an object for me, with no interiority. So I attempt to flee from the inescapable 'sadness' of responsibility and recognition—Klein's 'depressive position', Rose's 'sadness of the King'[11]—into a world of simple transparency, the visibility of myself to myself and of others to me. And the paradox is that the flight from sadness is what leads into catastrophe. Rose's analysis of what she terms sadness demonstrates that sadness is what permits a finally *comic* vision; it is the flight from sadness that precipitates tragedy.

But that is a paradox too far at this stage of the argument. What is coming into focus is the role in tragic representation of the refusal of the distinctively human forms of responsibility, grounded in the refusal of recognition. We refuse recognition to the other, and so refuse to recognize ourselves, our own implication in and with the other. And it is an act of recognition that is demanded of the audience to a tragic drama: in Cavell's words, a particular 'mode of perception' is asked of us that is unlike what occurs in response to other sorts of theatre[12] (we might say that this is because of tragedy's unequivocally liturgical roots; but more of that later). When we watch a tragic drama, we are deliberately immobilized; we cannot respond as we should do to human suffering in other circumstances. And this reinforces the recognition of *separateness*. 'What is revealed is my separateness from what is happening to them [the characters of the drama]; that I am I, and here.'[13] In this moment of my watching in the theatre, the only action that is going on is on the stage. I am both *free* from the necessity to act and *bound* to be still. I have surrendered this time to the action of others. And that, so Cavell argues, is where the tragic drama becomes transformative of my perception. I am enjoined as a spectator to *allow to happen what the tragic agents on stage are struggling not to allow*: I am affirming human separateness, the impenetrability of agents to each other, so that my/our response to suffering is to some degree stripped of the corrupting drama of easy identification with the sufferer, the absorption of the terrible otherness of alien pain into my own story. The agents in the drama—or at least the central 'tragic' figures, Othello or Lear or, indeed, Medea—draw the resistant and diverse reality of other agents into their own story, violently revenging themselves on those who will not let themselves be so absorbed; though they may in turn be the victims of the way others have already sought violently to absorb them (Othello as a character in the puppet play Iago constructs, Medea as victim of the self-interested suspension of law in Thebes). As Cavell implies, my immobilization in the face of terrible pain has here a contemplative quality; and when tragic liturgy has decayed or disappeared, we are left with a toxic gap in our human repertoire. Once, as audience to a tragic representation, we had a ceremonial 'doing nothing' which showed us why we feel helpless in the face of pain and loss—because we are still learning the solidarity that comes out of recognizing the sheer distance between actual human persons, so that our stillness in the face of represented pain becomes a forced acknowledgment of our habits of avoidance and denial and a confrontation of the helplessness in the presence of catastrophe that we regularly experience and avoid reflecting about. From this experience, we can recover a proper political ethic, we can learn better how and when to act. Without this liturgical moment, the only answer to the question of why we are doing nothing in the face of pain and terror—in the face, say, of constantly reported pain and terror, or pain and terror represented as entertaining anecdote; in the face of newsprint and screen—is that we have chosen to do nothing, a choice that 'requires the same energy, the same cunning and avoidance, that tragic activity used to have to itself'.[14] And the implication of *this* is that a culture without tragic drama, a culture in which the tragic audience has been replaced by the assembly of spectators, is itself exemplifying tragic disaster; it is refusing to know what it knows about humanity, and so is at risk of dying from what it does not know, like any classical tragic protagonist.

II

If tragedy is about the contemplation, the acknowledgement, of distance and inexhaustible dense 'solidity' in the other, if it is about the never-achieved level of steady attentiveness that we owe to each other, it must be saying something to us about how that debt is to be managed or realized, even if only by laying out the consequences of *not* paying the debt. At a crucial moment in *King Lear* (III.4), the king exclaims that 'Poor Tom', the naked madman, is 'the thing itself', the essential human being. 'Is man no more than this? Consider him well. Thou ow'st the worm no silk, the beast no hide, the sheep no wool, the cat no perfume…Thou art the thing itself: unaccommodated man is no more but such a poor bare, forked animal as thou art.' The key word is 'ow'st': Poor Tom is not in debt to anyone or anything. This is what it is to be an independent human agent. And the audience is prompted to think back to the whole trajectory of Lear's journey to this point. Part of the toughness of the play is its relentless exposure of Lear's confusion—even to the extent that the selfish and malicious daughters, Goneril and Regan, are allowed to speak the truth about him. He has begun (I.1) by claiming that he wants 'To shake all cares and business from our age' and 'crawl towards death' free from the burdens of responsibility; he looks forward to Cordelia's 'kind nursery' in his declining years. Yet he insists on the name and honours of royalty, and on his suite of knightly retainers: he appears to accept that he must be in debt to his family for care and nurture, but casts it as a debt that must be paid to himself, on his own terms. The model that is at work in the opening scene is a nakedly economic one: the debt of love is being called in by Lear, and the future of his daughters depends on how they discharge that debt, now and in the future; they must purchase their security by their articulation of love. What Lear is emphatically not doing is 'divesting' himself of authority in the way he claims, since he controls the currency of the exchange. Cordelia (and it is important not to sentimentalize the *prima facie* chill of her response) replies in exactly these terms, almost parodying their crassness: she loves *as is her duty*, she pays her debt: 'I return those duties back as are right fit.' And so Lear's confusion is once again pointed up: he has asked for—and he receives—payment of a debt; but what he wants is an assurance far beyond this. He wants to know that he is loved immeasurably beyond debt and duty, beyond the ordinary finite exchanges of 'due' affection or loyalty. Cordelia's blunt reminder that family affections run in many directions—that if she marries she will be bound to give half her love to her husband—is for Lear an offensive check to his fantasy of a love that is both at his disposal and immeasurable in its scope. He cannot manage with what is owed to him within the ordinary interdependence of human agents. It is a theme that recurs when he berates his daughters for their ingratitude when he has given them 'all' (II.2). His fantasy is that *he* has already made an immeasurable gift that now needs to be repaid in the same coin: 'Your old kind father whose frank heart gave all' (III.4). He cannot see his own love as limited, imperfect, and needy. As Regan has said in I.1, 'he hath ever but slenderly known himself'.

When his demands are rejected by both his elder daughters, and he is wandering in the storm, he initially feels the stirrings of something like ordinary compassion: 'How dost, my boy? Art cold?/ I am cold myself' (III.2). He recognizes that he has 'ta'en/ Too little care of this' (III.4), and that his present misery has exposed him to what need actually consists in for most human beings. But the interruption of the discovery of Poor Tom seems to push him back into his obsessional talk of ingratitude. 'Has his daughters brought him to this pass?/ Couldst thou save nothing? Wouldst thou give 'em all?' And this leads to the climactic 'Is man no more than this?' Lear has struggled to define the mutual debt of human agents in his terms—his own giving of love seen as unconditional and the debt in return being unconditional and irrational (un-'lawful', we could say); what he cannot countenance is finite relationship, genuine mutual dependence. And now here is a human figure who has given 'all' away, and who has no debts to discharge: the thing itself—both in the sense of 'the height of style or propriety' and in the sense of the pure *object*—a reality existing always and only in the third person, devoid of reciprocity. The passionate nihilism of this vision persists into the harrowing dialogue with blind Gloucester in IV.5, with its furious repudiation of the whole language of debt, merit, earned well-being: 'None does offend, none, I say, none.' In a world where evil is not repaid for evil and greed and corruption flourish without punishment, there will always be a way to 'seal th'accuser's lips'. Nothing is 'owed' to human beings simply for what they are; immunity from punishment can always be bought. In place of a network of mutual need, what characterizes human society is the calculation of purchasing power. The economic language of the opening scene comes back with a vengeance: there is only the market—not even the partially disguised, collusive 'market' of comforting words that is invoked in the opening scene, but the naked buying of safety and well-being and public immunity, with nothing for those who lack purchasing power.

But just as Cordelia in the first scene of the play exposes, with dour insistence, the underlying logic—and lack of logic—in Lear's demands, so here she is brought in precisely to challenge this dystopic frame of reference. In IV.6, as she prepares to wake her father, she reflects that his age and frailty alone should have guaranteed his safety at the hands of her sisters. She appeals to an inchoate level of compassion that goes beyond even family sympathy, even sympathy to a fellow human being: 'Mine enemy's dog, though he had bit me/ Should have stood that night against my fire.' Lear, waking, declares his willingness to be punished by Cordelia:'If you have poison for me, I will drink it./ I know you do not love me. For your sisters/ Have, as I remember, done me wrong:/ You have some cause, they have not.' She cannot possibly love him; he has earned nothing and Cordelia owes him nothing. He has no purchase on her. But she protests that she has 'No cause, no cause' to injure him: she reaffirms the natural compassion Lear had begun to sense in the storm, the simple pity for human or beast that compels hospitality. She has already reaffirmed, in a phrase with strongly biblical resonance, that she is indeed, unalterably, Lear's child ('and so I am, I am'), and that her duty is rooted not in a calculation of merit but in the bare fact of connection. The independent agent, owing nothing, has been left exposed, naked, on the storm-ravaged heath and is here left behind; the 'invested' agent, always implicated in the other before there is any choice or negotiation about it, is reinstated.

Cordelia's words and actions in this scene allow us to re-read her initial response to her father's demands. He has asked at the play's opening for the repayment of a debt he has calculated in terms of what he imagines he has given ('I gave you all', he says later in the play): the imagined opulence of his gift of love lays on the recipients an obligation that he believes should properly challenge and exercise the rhetorical resources of his daughters. What he does not expect is that it should turn out to be literally inexpressible. Goneril—as A. D. Nuttall notes in his brief and penetrating discussion of the play[15]— begins with the 'inexpressibility topos' ('I love you more than words can wield the matter')—which means that Cordelia cannot even say what she can't say: it is as if the currency of inarticulacy as well as of articulacy has been debased by Goneril's theatrical foreclosure. Lear's fictional unreserved generosity draws out from Goneril a fictional response of 'inexpressible' love. Cordelia is left with only the option of insisting that her love is as it should be on the grounds of her connection with her father, no more, no less, as she says. If we are going to speak of debts—she implies—then the level of 'payment' is simply a *given*. Price and value are not to be haggled over, and there is no possible ground for a bidding war in love. And what we hear her saying in IV.6 allows us to interpret her earlier words more adequately. The interdependence of human love is indeed 'immeasurable', but not in the sense that Lear imagines: the identity of each and all is grounded in an indebtedness that cannot be quantified, since it is simply a function of our being located where we are in a world, with the actual interdependence we have. The person who fantasizes *either* that he or she can make unlimited demands as a matter of right *or* (which comes, Shakespeare suggests, to the same thing) that there can be a human life free of 'owing' is destined for tragic catastrophe. The debt under which we all lie is what belongs to a common condition in which we cannot live without recognizing what we need from the human other, in family or in society. The debt-free individual is the one who has no intelligible speech left, nothing to share, the 'naked wretch' who appears to Lear as the dark mirror of his own fictions.

The idea that I can dispense or receive love without limit is both the most dangerous of fantasies and the most fundamental of truths; *Lear* is in part about the appalling difficulty of telling the difference between unconditional love as limitless benevolence demanding or earning limitless repayment and unconditional love as that which is always there in advance and never open to negotiation. To move from the former to the latter is to move by way of dispossession: love has to be affirmed irrespective equally of merit and of outcomes. What makes this probably the most challenging of Shakespeare's plays is that, while we may be able to get our minds around the former, the latter is dismaying. We arrive at a precarious moral vantage point in IV.6, with Cordelia's compassion and Lear's penitence; and it is as though Shakespeare then says to the audience: 'I am now going to kill these two characters; will what they have said or seen still be true?' And, as Nuttall points out,[16] it is not only that the deeply moving reconciliation is followed by more suffering; it is also that the Lear who kills Cordelia's executioner is not obviously someone who has internalized a gospel of forgiveness and regeneration. Shakespeare is clearly not interested in a consoling ending of any sort, but equally it is not obvious that the ending is in itself a refutation of what has happened before. There is more suffering; but who said that Lear's pain would be over when he was reconciled with Cordelia? There is a reversion to vengeance; but who said that Lear had become a saint? The questions left are whether the play's underlying diagnosis of (some of) the roots of suffering in denial and fiction is true, and whether the reconciliation of Lear and Cordelia, and Lear's partial regeneration, are any less significant for being transient. This is a tragic drama which announces that *time goes on*: we are never going to be in a position to say that pain is now over—as indeed Edgar recognizes when he is first brought face to face with his blinded father (IV.1): 'The worst is not/ So long as we can say "This is the worst".' It is a phrase which should be taken as Shakespeare's warning to his audience not to expect any temporal easing or resolution of the suffering of his chief characters. No reconciliation on this personal scale will be adequate to the unreconciled reality that prevails all around and that may once again intrude into the lives of the reconciled. 'This is the worst' is a statement that seeks to close down the history of suffering; now we know how bad it can be. But the drama declares that we do not know how bad it can be, and that this is one of those things we must *know* that we don't know. Before Gloucester appears, Edgar has just come out with a bland 'wheel of fortune' bromide, concluding 'Welcome, then,/ Thou unsubstantial air that I embrace!/ The wretch that thou hast blown unto the worst/ *Owes* nothing to thy blasts.' He imagines that, after a patch of acute humiliation and misery, a debt has been cleared: whatever it is that malign fate or divine justice demands in terms of suffering has now been dealt with and the slate is clear. But the model of debt and repayment works no better here than it does with the exchanges of love. There is no guaranteed settling of scores, no promise of an 'earned' security or repose. Lear declares that he will 'take upon [him] the mystery of things' (V.3); but the burden he literally takes on himself is the dead body of Cordelia.

The tragic imagination is in this sense inimical to the most obvious versions of reconciliation, though not, as we shall see a little later, to all. The business of tragedy is neither to tell us that the world is more bearable than it is nor to insist that it is 'absolutely' unbearable. It is a more problematic and unsettling matter than any such generalization, in that it shows us how *some* pain can be spoken of and understood, 'humanized', and some cannot, because the words are not yet there and, so far as we can know, may never be; and we also cannot know what the level of pain or horror is that is to come. If there is some way of thinking or speaking of disproportionate and terrible pain that is not bland or illusory, it is nothing to do with the relieved sense that we have now *come to know* something. There is no intellectual progress over the millennia in theories about the problem of suffering as there may be in theories about the birth of stars or the working of the brain.

III

So one essential aspect of the tragic imagination, we might say, is to clarify what sort of 'knowledge' it is that we acquire in respect of suffering. Tragic drama returns us to the specific moment of suffering or the specific subject of suffering and presents us with a particularly sharp paradox: it has proved possible to represent this specific moment; here we are repeating it, holding it before an audience as something that can be in some sense known. But: what is being represented is itself a moment or a subject always about to be overtaken by events that cannot be controlled; knowing the suffering represented is also knowing that it is *human* suffering, 'historical' suffering if you like. Narrating in the drama *this* particular moment of pain makes something possible for an audience in their own specific moment and subjectivity. It is the possibility of contemplating suffering without complete inarticulacy or despair, *thinking* about pain in a way that allows us to feel not completely passive in the face of the world's menace. But that contemplation has a price: this is suffering about which we cannot make any difference, fixed in the narrative as we are fixed in our seats as spectators. We are made both to sense that we are not passive and to recognize that there is no action open to us except words and reflection. We cannot change the narrative for those who are involved in it. What then can we change? Presumably our own repertoire of responses to pain in ourselves or each other. And that involves a rather ironic kind of change—coming to recognize what we don't know and can't say. What we learn in tragedy is a familiarity with what *can't* be, in the ordinary sense, learned. Tragedy does not provide mastery of a skill, fluency in an area of discourse. What happens is that we become—or, more realistically, we are taken some small distance on the journey to becoming—subjects who know that they will always be confronted with suffering that cannot be controlled, their own and that of others; which is one way of saying that we know ourselves to be historical subjects who cannot change the past or guarantee the future.

But I have suggested that *Lear* allows us to know a little more than that alone, though it is a disputable kind of knowing. Pain can be represented; and *shared* pain can be represented. At that highly charged moment in *Lear* when the captured king and Cordelia are brought before Edmund (V.3), Cordelia says: 'For thee, oppressed king, am I cast down:/ Myself could else out-frown false fortune's frown.' Tragedy represents not only the pain of individuals but, in various ways, the effect of such pain on witnesses—whether it is in the shocked or traumatized comments and responses of a Greek chorus, or, as here, in the still more marked form of an agent and sufferer within the drama setting aside their own pain in the contemplation of another's. It is an intensification of moments earlier in the play (III.2) when Lear turns to the Fool with compassion ('Art cold?/ I am cold myself ... Poor fool and knave, I have one part in my heart/ That's sorry yet for thee'), or when the blinded Gloucester expresses his pity both for Edgar and for Poor Tom in IV.1, and speaks, with what must be a frisson of self-recognition, of the man 'who will not see/ Because he cannot feel.' And the terrible encounter between Lear and Gloucester in IV.5 has already shown us how one person's pain can be pushed out of focus by another's, as Gloucester responds with horror and pity to Lear's madness. Cordelia, as often in the play, provides a clear, almost prosaic statement of currents that are circulating close beneath the surface.

The force of this is to say that part of what we know as a result of the drama is what is known by sufferers within the drama *about each other*. Drama does not simply depict solitary pain; just as it brings pain into language for us as audience, it shows language finding its way in handling pain within its own boundaries; it shows us what is said by sufferers and about other sufferers. It represents different kinds of *witnessing* to pain, one of which is the 'self-displacement' shown by Cordelia, and to a lesser extent Gloucester and even Lear. We know as audience that witnessing another's acute pain can suspend our self-obsessions for an hour or so, that we can be held in a degree of stillness by witnessing the drama. But the drama also tells us that even the most acute pain and loss is not necessarily *closed off* to the pain of another: the sufferer can still know and even vicariously sense what another is enduring ('I have one part in my heart ...'). If one aspect of tragic representation is simply the affirmation that something can be spoken rather than locked in total silence, beyond words and meaning, another is that experiencing extreme pain does not automatically make one deaf to the atrocity another is experiencing. 'I should e'en die with pity/ To see another thus', Lear muses as he wakes in Cordelia's presence (IV.6). It is a significant feature of Shakespeare's tragic framework; we shall be looking in a later chapter at what more recent dramatists do with it. In *Lear* he both deliberately ratchets up the level of atrocity (Gloucester's blinding on stage) and, at least in the Quarto text, intensifies the risky compassion of Cornwall's servants, who, although they have seen one of their number killed trying to defend Gloucester, still co-operate in helping the old man.

This is not to claim that moments of compassion soften the bleakness of a tragic situation or point to transcendental resolutions. Gloucester is still blind, and the horror of the blinding scene is ineradicable; nothing can make the world a place where these things do not happen. What is at issue is simply the way suffering can be known, within the terms and relations of the drama, by sufferers; so that what we know as audience is not just the record of an individual in agony but the kind of communication (perhaps sometimes—but not automatically—solidarity) that arises in the wake of terrible and disproportionate pain. Grigori Kozintsev's film of *Lear* visualizes this point starkly by setting the agonies of the main characters against the backdrop of large groups of the displaced and dishonoured poor: the sufferings of Lear, Gloucester, and others bring into focus a 'deep background' normally invisible to the main actors.[17] The action of the play culminates in just that sort of 'exposure' that Lear speaks of in III.4 as he begins his wandering in the storm ('Expose thyself to feel what wretches feel'). And this reinforces the conclusion that the tragic dramatist is engaged in putting into words something of that mutual *recognition* so emphasized by Gillian Rose as the core of the ethical. A drama in which every experience of pain was unrecognized within the drama itself, in which there was no communication between the characters about (or within?) pain, would be one where the dramatist alone would be charged with the burden of the ethical in Rose's sense: only the dramatist would *speak* of pain, only the dramatist would point towards solidarity. But a drama is a linguistic exchange; what it makes visible is pain as something that can be communicated about, pain as a 'cultural' fact. What the audience of tragic drama witnesses is what suffering does to human exchanges, to language and understanding, not simply the raw fact of pain. And this, of course, *accentuates* the challenge of suffering rather than softening it. As an ethical challenge it has to do with what makes it possible in situations of terrible pain to recognize another—to recognize the sufferer as a human speaker with a history and an intelligible narrative, to recognize that another's suffering has an impact on my own, is not alien to my own. Tragic drama, by staging these sorts of recognition, tells its audience that their task is to find a way of knowing pain that is grounded in recognition of the kind enacted before them.

And, as a further ironic reminder that knowledge in itself is not going to do the job, Shakespeare elsewhere demonstrates how there is a knowledge of another's pain, a kind of recognition that is both genuinely truthful and deeply poisonous. Iago knows about the pain of others; he is a supremely empathetic villain, planning the destruction of Othello with a subtle awareness of *what it is like* to be Othello. His 'seduction' of Othello—as we can reasonably call it—into insane suspicion is carefully calibrated, working with the grain of an overheated sexual imagination which Iago indulges skilfully (III.3: 'You would be satisfied [of the truth of Iago's suspicions]?...How satisfied, my lord?/ Would you the supervision grossly gape on? Behold her topped?'). He 'reads' the behaviour of those around from Othello's distorted point of view (IV.1, 'As he shall smile, Othello shall go mad'), imagining himself further into the world he has helped to create: he manipulates a genuine but misplaced emotion into position, then works from that fantasy-dominated point of view. Iago is among many other things a diabolical image of the dramatist: he 'stages' suffering, knowing its workings in the mind of an other. As Nuttall says, 'Othello's murderous passion is formed in the relational space between persons, by the public medium of words audible to us, the watchers of the play';[18] or, to put it slightly differently, Othello's passion is imagined into existence in that cultural space where suffering is thought about and spoken about, and which generates dramas of suffering. Iago is the one who draws together the language-based knowledge, the cultural knowledge, of passion and pain into a 'plot', because he has heard and attended to Othello and to the received cultural models of jealousy and sexual obsession. He tests these out in himself, reporting (I.3) that Othello is believed to have cuckolded him and, in effect, decides that this will be the role he chooses to play, deciding to pretend jealousy. He 'knows' the pain of sexual envy, knows how it works or is imagined to work as a comprehensible cultural excuse for hatred. He creates his dramatic role as he creates a role for Othello.

So the audience is prompted to recognize something further of what they know and do not know about pain: there is a knowing of pain that can be instrumentalized so as to contain or control others. As spectators, we have to come to terms with the fact that what we are learning as we watch the tragic drama can be an induction into awareness of the proper inaccessibility of another's suffering, never fathomed, never adequately seen or represented—or it may be turned, by one of the most obvious seductions of art, into a means of consolidating our spectator's position—understanding, like Iago, the working of pain but using this understanding to avoid solidarity, participation. The drama shows us communication in pain between sufferers, challenging any idea that pain is essentially or necessarily beyond language; but once that is granted, we also have to grant that it may be *mis*represented in language in the sense that it can be rendered 'available' for manipulation. Othello at the end of the play (V.2) asks of Iago 'Why he hath thus ensnared my soul and body?', receiving the famous reply, 'Demand me nothing: what you know, you know.' This response is not only, as Cavell so eloquently argues, an almost mocking reminder to Othello that he has been attempting to know in a way no human can know; it is also a defiant accusation, aimed at Othello and others on stage—and presumably the audience as well. Why do we seek to 'ensnare' one another? We know the answer: we know enough of the reality of another's emotion to be tempted to make them work in our own dramas. A figure like Iago, with unusual awareness of how or where others are vulnerable to suffering, can carry this through with more devastating effect than most, but we all (we, the audience) know the urge to capture the emotions of another for our own dramas. Tragic representation can show both a recognition that delivers us from an imprisoning self-concern and a recognition that reinforces our self-concern by helping us draw others into our 'scripts'. 'What you know, you know': what we do not want to acknowledge that we know is our *recognition* of Iago. We shouldn't need to ask why Iago behaves as he does—or so he is telling us.

If all this is correct, certain central aspects of tragic representation come into focus, and it is worth pausing to identify them. Tragic drama engages in three interwoven tasks of unmasking or uncovering, and invites us to do some mental and moral discrimination around the idea of knowledge. Tragedy, first of all, as Cavell stresses, makes us *sit still and do nothing*. It denies us the chance of intervening in horrific and traumatic events, so that we better understand our own habitual denials and refusals of involvement. We need to grasp that the pain we see represented is absolutely not ours, that it belongs in a situation that we cannot change, cannot make acceptable to ourselves or controllable by ourselves. We are reduced to being witnesses; the fixity of the dramatic narrative holds us at a distance from the pain we see, so that we are forced to see it as other and so as demanding a particular kind of attention. At this primary level, what tragedy teaches us is the sheer discipline of holding back and not intruding as either messiahs or fellow-sufferers. It discloses the risk and the power of denial, of refusing to know the unknowability of another's suffering.

Then there is a second level, crucially sketched for us in some aspects of *Lear*, as we have seen. The pain we witness is a pain that is visible in its context, spoken of, shared in certain ways. Most positively, it is shared in compassion; some who literally share a condition of suffering allow themselves to be affected by the pain of others, judge and even relativize their own suffering in the light of the neighbour's pain. But even where there is no radical compassion of this sort, the suffering of agents in the drama draws in the comment and response of others; it is a public and linguistic or cultural reality. What we see in the drama is a narrative in which pain does not finally close off the sufferer from understanding and being understood. Tragedy typically displays the agonizing isolation of the person in pain, but, in the very fact of displaying it *to* an audience and *within* the conversation of the drama, the dramatist displays suffering as something that can be spoken of, and even to. The disturbance of tragedy is not the revelation that suffering is beyond words but the unwelcome insight that suffering is bound up with the most extreme *difficulty* of words; that we need to go on trying to describe (Akhmatova once more) what resists description. The impetus to go on trying is reinforced by the way in which a drama *makes language out of pain*; and this entails something other than complete despair in the face of pain, because the drama displays some responses to pain that are not simply self-protective. We learn that suffering calls out recognition.

But the third level immediately qualifies any merely optimistic take on this. Making language out of pain means that representing suffering is as liable as any other form of discourse to be ideologically captured, selfishly or manipulatively deployed, used as a tool of power or as a vehicle of consolation by those whose ideologies or anxieties make them prone to evasions of the tragic. The very features that give tragic drama its moral significance also endow it with moral risk. A tragedy like *Othello* shows us that there can be a sharing of the understanding of pain that is open to being deployed for the sake of controlling and damaging another. It is possible to use tragic narrative to create or reinforce power. You can speak with understanding, even interiority, about pain, and still be instrumentalizing the sufferer, drawing them into a drama that is about your own concerns and aspirations. You can, like Iago, use insight and imagination to intensify another's humiliation and ensnarement. And a tragic drama that works morally is going to be one that stages this risk as sharply as it stages the possibilities of compassion, a drama that directs to its audience the kind of challenge that Iago's last words on stage imply. If it fails to do this, it becomes another tool for mystifying or obscuring knowledge; it will teach us to *ignore*—when one of the central purposes of tragedy, as we have outlined it, is to insist that we do not ignore (our ignorance, our longing for disengagement, our longing for control).

Three tasks, or three phases of one task, which is to clarify what it is to know human suffering justly or properly, knowing its absolute specificity and inaccessibility to the non-sufferer but also its representability and so its capacity to be in some sense or measure shared, within a drama's action, between dramatic characters and audience, in visceral sympathy or in fear; and then knowing that representation itself always needs to be scrutinized for any sign of a return to an agenda that seeks deliberately partial, 'useful', knowledge of pain. At this point, we might recall Gillian Rose's cautions, quoted towards the end of chapter 1, about what is represented at Auschwitz. She identifies the dangers both of a too easy solidarity and of a too easy individualized remorse, and insists that we turn the question towards institutions—that is, towards those public practices and discourses that shape corporate action and corporate judgement.[19] A knowledge of suffering that is simply a frisson of 'There but for the grace of God ...' is unsettling in the wrong way, reducing the issue to one of individual or local insecurity. A knowledge that induces (sentimental) individual guilt is inadequate to the scale of a corporate human failure of unparalleled proportions—though this is not to dismiss the integrity of solitary refusal and resistance. And, in the light of the discussions in this chapter, we could add, a knowledge that amounts to the claim to have an understanding of suffering *to hand*—in a way that allows us to use it just for the reinforcement of a position or an agenda—is a tacit denial or refusal of the unexhausted strangeness of another's pain. Tragedy invites us (at best compels us) to ask what a language about suffering would sound like that did not just embody these sorts of knowledge— granted that because disproportionate pain is *difficult* to look at and speak of, most speech about it is going to be shadowed by these distortions.

We judge the integrity and effect of a tragic text or performance by the degree to which we leave—or look up, we might say, with an echo of *Lear*—with a consciousness of unfinished business. There is the unfinishable business of looking at what we will never have looked at enough, and the business of speaking of it in ways that do not imply closure and control. There is also the business of examining the culture we inhabit (the institutions we inhabit) for signs of the individual and collective instrumentalizing of suffering—whether by absorbing it into defensive narratives about ourselves or by an aesthetic display of empathetic understanding. Tragic discourse, tragic drama, could in this light be seen as an essentially *intelligent* response to pain, to the degree that intelligence makes possible more not less looking and more not less effort to free what we are looking at from our internal dramas and fancies. It is something rather like this, I think, that Susan Sontag implies towards the close of her impassioned but tantalizingly diffuse essay on *Regarding the Pain of Others* when she argues that we should be careful about too global a moral judgement on the evils of looking at images of suffering. It is true that there is something very ambiguous about the way such images are presented in the media; but the problem does not lie in *images* of suffering. 'Watching up close—without the mediation of an image—is still just watching.'[20] And if we feel that 'we pay too high a human (or moral) price' for the legendary clarity that we associate with seeing, as opposed to the other senses, we should reflect that this is a little like complaining about the clarity of thinking as such. If vision enables a 'standing back from the aggressiveness of the world which frees us for observation and elective attention', what it enables is 'the function of the mind itself'.[21] 'There's nothing wrong', she concludes, 'with standing back and thinking. To paraphrase several sages: "Nobody can think and hit at the same time." '[22]

But in fact Sontag's discussion brings into better focus some of what it is that drama alone can do. There is a difference between looking at images of pain and the kind of looking involved in watching a drama: we can always close our eyes, but the drama continues to address our senses in other ways. We have discussed some of what Stanley Cavell says about the enforced silence and relative stillness entailed by being in an audience as a condition for *reflection*; as such it effectively holds us back for the moment from any action that could either intensify or relieve the pain that we are witnessing. But there is more. Sontag grants earlier in her essay that our looking at an image of suffering will be regularly interpreted with an instant moral charge if the suffering is of someone from 'my' party ('what matters is precisely who is killed and by whom').[23] An image so interpreted becomes a reinforcement of what I believe (and who it is that I hate). But the drama is a mobile image that has the capacity to challenge this: images of pain are—as we have observed—spoken, seen, interpreted among speakers. It is harder for any image of suffering to be just a reinforcement, and so the tragic drama is more securely connected than the static picture with what Sontag calls 'the function of the mind itself'. The dramatizing both of compassion and of the seduction of what I have called 'empathic manipulation' locates the pain that is imaged within the cultural exchanges of language and power; that is the distinctive contribution of the theatre. And a drama that for some reason avoided or marginalized either of these issues would be less than properly tragic; it would be reaching out to the emotions that a static image might look to. It might not necessarily be corrupt or ineffective, but, as Sontag argues, it would be a more obviously shadowed affair.

As we come away from the tragic drama, the knowledge we have gained is not simply a knowledge that the world is terrible, that waste and suffering are finally inescapable and beyond healing, or even that we cannot ever think that the story of human pain is over and done with. All of these are accompaniments of a knowledge of suffering that is more complex—not as such more hopeful or more despairing, but simply more intertwined with our linguistic practice. In tragedy, we know pain as something that can be shared—not in a way that automatically eases it or ends it, let alone 'justifying' it, but simply as something that features in the relationships that we speak and think about. And so we also know pain as something the knowledge of which can be deployed in the struggles for power and advantage. If we did not in some sense recognize each other's pain, if we had no capacity for compassion, we should not have the possibility of Iago's intelligent calculation of Othello's pain, and the terrible struggle for advantage that this generates. As spectators, we are reminded of our potential complicity with this; the good dramatist admits her or his own complicity in the way a drama handles this.

IV

Shakespeare presents us with the protest of *Lear* against an imagined moral world in which human interaction can be measured in terms of debt and satisfaction, and lays out for us the lethal consequences of the refusals involved in trying to live consistently in such a world. We imagine a paradigmatic humanity as one delivered from debt, owing nothing to anyone; and we are shown that a 'debt-free' humanity is naked and incoherent. Our relations are not bits of finite moral/emotional capital to be exchanged in a tidy market of obligation. The way in which our words and our silences create or destroy relations is far more anarchic than that. And so it is not surprising that we encounter responses to the suffering of another that represent both the acknowledgement of a debt far beyond any capacity of satisfactory payment, a debt of unreserved attention and love, and an excess of involvement, care, disregarding calculation altogether; all this is what Cordelia embodies.

But Shakespeare also presents us with the *risk* of representing suffering. We can imagine the suffering of another; and (assuming we happen not to be Cordelia) we can use that imagining to contain and control another. The dramatist, who is, of course, imagining suffering, has to confront the questions that might be asked about what it means to create a human subject in words and then to destroy them; and the dramatist who asks this of himself or herself will also throw to the audience (and, indeed, to the critic, the interpreter, the would-be philosopher of tragedy) the question of what it means to absorb narratives and representations of suffering if we happen not to be Cordelia.

What are we to do with our knowledge? It can be transformed into a sentimental self-awareness, a fascination with our own vulnerability; it can be turned into a troublingly lucid awareness of how we might secure ourselves against others or consolidate our advantage over others, even destroy the threat of others. And so it makes sense to conclude that what we come to know about suffering through the medium of tragic drama will need to be located within a larger context than simply the knowledge of suffering; we have to develop some account of how this knowledge is grounded in, and itself informs, our knowledge of human reflection as such ('the function of the mind itself').

In the next chapter we shall be looking at what Hegel has to say about tragedy. It is important to stress from the start that Hegel's thinking on this subject is very far from being a kind of 'outcrop' of his system; as we shall see, it is a subject that is bound up with the most central aspects of what he has to say about 'the function of the mind'. The knowledge of suffering that we have been reflecting on in this chapter is, in Hegel's schema, a gateway into knowledge of what it is to think at all. It is not just that—as in the famous Aeschylean phrase[24]—knowledge comes through suffering, in the sense that knowledge teaches us hard and necessary lessons; rather, suffering tells us something about knowledge itself, and tragic narrative becomes an inseparable part of any epistemology. The tragic narrative/representation requires not simply an emotional response of empathy, nor a deepened level of emotional literacy. These are ambivalent things, they may even be corrupting things, given our propensity to use them for security or advantage. For the tragic text or performance to do its work, it requires us to follow through to those buried levels of awareness—what the American philosopher Walter Davis calls 'the crypt'[25]—where our most significant human dysfunctions are rooted. Davis argues that the tragic is intrinsically opposed to the experience of 'enthusiasm'—the embrace of an event that secures the satisfying discharge of conflicted feeling,[26] catharsis in the simplest sense of a delivery from the feeling of doubt, anguish, or the absence of guarantee. A drama that sets out to provide such an 'event' will in fact deny the tragic even when claiming to embody it. For Davis, the simplistic understanding of tragic catharsis as primarily *release* from tension is one of the foremost enemies of the genuinely tragic; it confuses the purgation of the ego that tragedy insists upon in its audience with a sort of therapy of self-expression, 'discharging' in the sense of 'letting it all out' and so restoring a (basically fictional or illusory) harmony. What is articulated in the tragic is 'negative capability' of a depth that can sustain the dissolving of triumph, hope, reconciliation, the solid and justified ego. It demands the loss of the self.

There is a good deal more to be said about Davis's uncompromising account, but our present point is to do with how tragedy challenges our relation to ourselves at the most fundamental level. In the first chapter, we reflected on the way in which Greek tragedy both insisted on the necessity of our identification within the city for our humanity to be secure and made visible the diverse vulnerabilities of the civic order. The audience has to understand that its shared identity is necessary and fragile: ignore the necessity and you are left with lawless rivalry and unlimited revenge, with the lack of mutual recognition; ignore the fragility and you are left with the kind of illusion that can lead to another sort of lawlessness, the positivism of a power beyond challenge. In the present chapter, the focus has been on two issues: tragedy as reacquainting us with our own contingency, with the unknowability of what we may have to face coming from within or without ourselves; and the question of what we need in order to *think* about pain, waste, and loss. We have been looking at the ways in which tragedy 'immobilizes' us and forces us to be silent before the other in their suffering, but also at how tragedy—especially Shakespearean tragedy—warns against corrupt ways of knowing such suffering. In both respects, the tragic representations we have been examining here echo classical tragedy's concerns about *power*, especially unexamined power. The risks of unexamined political power (of a politics that has lost sight of its roots in the management of revenge and rivalry and in the consequent necessity for lawful recognition of one another) are, in Shakespeare, sometimes transferred directly, as in the central history plays and in some aspects of *Lear*, and sometimes translated into the terms of personal power and the aspiration to a complete absorption of the other, as elsewhere in the capacious landscape of *Lear*, in *Othello*, and (though it is not technically a tragedy) in *The Winter's Tale*. The basic questions carry through—about recognition, justice, self-delusion, the refusal to know, the need to acknowledge the stranger. Tragic narrative is, in one way or another, the story of what happens when these things are ignored.

And so it is the story of a reconstituted self as much as of a reconstituted city (as in Greek drama): familiar with its fragility, knowing better what it is to know or understand. I suggested earlier that tragedy could be seen as the way we learn to be 'intelligent' about suffering without yielding to the temptation to use that intelligence for the good of the unreconstructed ego. Insofar as this must mean a continuing challenge to that ego, tragedy is indeed the key to a different mode of thinking. For Davis, this is a thinking that arises from the 'passion' involved in digging down to the level of affect where our habitual forms of self-relatedness are buried;[27] as we excavate these roots and 'deracinate' our familiar self-constructions, we become 'psyche', a self that is held in the presence of its own pain and disorder, refusing to return to a sanitized and reconciled world. This is 'the process of infecting ourselves with ourselves in order to take action within ourselves';[28] this is thinking. And for Davis this inverts the Hegelian process by which conflict is brought to order. Davis reads Hegel as thinking of a self that is constituted by self-mediation in which tension is continuously being discharged in the activity of thought: we begin with one picture of self and world, are driven to its rational or logical opposite and then find, in opposing that opposition, a resting-place for thought. But Davis's understanding of self-mediation is a progression into deeper and deeper levels of affective crisis and contradiction, so as to deliver us from one or another kind of denial of the world and of the actual and contingent self.

Once again, we encounter a particular reading of Hegel on tragedy which, like Nussbaum's, assumes that Hegelian reconciliation delivers a spuriously consistent human history and human self. It is time to ask whether this is indeed Hegel's understanding—and, if not, how he constructs a tragic self that is 'held' honestly in the presence of pain and disorder, rather than being in metaphysical flight from it.

Notes

1. Augustine, *Confessions*, translated by Henry Chadwick, Oxford University Press 1991, X.xvii (26), p.194.
2. Ibid., viii (15), p.187.
3. References by page and line number to *Oedipus the King*, in *Sophocles: The Three Theban Plays*, translated by Robert Fagles, Harmondsworth, Penguin Classics 1984 (revised).

4. Cavell's major systematic work on philosophy is *The Claim of Reason: Wittgenstein, Skepticism, Morality and Tragedy*, Oxford University Press 1979; Part Four, 'Skepticism and the Problem of Others', subtitled 'Between Acknowledgment and Avoidance' is particularly important for his reflections on tragedy.
5. Cavell, *The Claim of Reason*, p.496.
6. Ibid., pp.481–96; also published as 'Othello and the Stake of the Other' in Stanley Cavell, *Disowning Knowledge in Seven Plays of Shakespeare*, Cambridge University Press 1987, updated 2003, pp.125–42. Further references are to this latter version.
7. Cavell, *Disowning Knowledge*, p.138.
8. Ibid., p.141.
9. Gillian Rose, *Judaism and Modernity: Philosophical Essays*, Oxford, Blackwell 1993, p.35.
10. Gillian Rose, *Mourning Becomes the Law: Philosophy and Representation*, Cambridge University Press 1996, p.75.
11. Gillian Rose, *Love's Work*, London, Chatto and Windus 1995, p.115. See Rowan Williams, '"The Sadness of the King": Gillian Rose, Hegel and the Pathos of Reason', *Telos* 173 (Winter 2015).
12. Cavell, *Disowning Knowledge*, p.91.
13. Ibid., p.109.
14. Ibid., p.117.
15. A. D. Nuttall, *Shakespeare the Thinker*, Yale University Press 2007, p.304.
16. Ibid., p.306.
17. For Kozintsev's own reflections on this, see his diary of the making of the film: *King Lear: The Space of Tragedy*, London, Heinemann Educational Publishers 1977.
18. Nuttall, *Shakespeare the Thinker*, p.281.
19. Gillian Rose, ' "The Future of Auschwitz" ', *Judaism and Modernity*, pp.33–6.
20. Susan Sontag, *Regarding the Pain of Others*, London, Hamish Hamilton 2003, p.105.
21. Ibid. p.106.
22. Ibid., pp.105–6.
23. Ibid., p.9.
24. *Agamemnon*, 177.
25. Walter Davis, *Deracination: Historicity, Hiroshima and the Tragic Imperative*, Albany NY, SUNY Press 2001, especially chapter 4.
26. Ibid., pp.165ff.
27. Ibid., pp.180, 183.
28. Ibid., p.182.

3

Reconciliation and its Discontents

Thinking with Hegel

I

Hegel's paradigm tragedy is Sophocles' *Antigone*—a text to which he returns in several different contexts, from his early writings to the *Phenomenology*, and eventually the 1827 *Lectures on the Philosophy of Religion*.[1] In his lectures on the fine arts, he describes it as 'the most excellent and satisfying work of art'.[2] What fascinates Hegel in this drama is the presentation of two inflexible expressions of law which cannot both be satisfied—or rather, which cannot be satisfied without destroying the lives of the agents who take responsibility for honouring them. It forms the final act of the Oedipus story—though the play itself was the first to be written of the Sophoclean trilogy of Theban dramas: Creon becomes ruler of Thebes once Oedipus is dead and his sons, Eteocles and Polynices, have killed each other fighting over the succession; and the narrative of the play deals with the aftermath of this struggle. Creon orders that the corpse of Polynices should lie unburied, since he has attacked the city itself, with the help of other Greek warlords, while Eteocles receives an honourable funeral. Disobedience to this order will be punished with death. Polynices' sister Antigone declares that, as a member of his family, she intends to fulfil her sacred obligations to the dead, and to accord Polynices the proper rites of burial he has been denied. Creon condemns her to death, although she is engaged to his son, Haemon; when the seer Tiresias rebukes Creon for his obstinacy, he eventually consents both to bury Polynices and to reprieve Antigone, but arrives too late at the place where Antigone has been immured alive. She has hanged herself; Haemon turns on his father, intending to kill him, but then kills himself. In the wake of this, Creon's wife, Eurydice, also commits suicide. Creon is left alone and devastated: he describes himself as 'no-one' and 'nothing' (126.1446).[3] He prays for death, but is told by the Leader of the Chorus, 'No more prayers now. For mortal men/ there is no escape from the doom we must endure' (127.1457–8).

How is it possible that human beings should have to face imperatives that are not compatible? Hegel's reading of this conundrum is that *Antigone* presents us with a specific stage of human self-awareness in which the human recognition of the self as thinking, as constructing the continuities within its operation, is still bound to a particular kind of external image. Spirit, the life of thinking, 'appears' in the form of a compellingly attractive divine presence over against the subject, and the subject seeks to be conformed to this beautiful and harmonious presence, which exists *for* the subject's consciousness.[4] The ethical/ spiritual capacity of the subject is already activated (without this there would be no impulse to be in harmony with the beautiful), so that the inner life is already developing; but it is still configured in terms of image, externality, the abstract turned into a specific, locally discernible 'sacred' which makes its demands on the self. What then happens is that the incipiently self-conscious subject *identifies* itself with the image of free and ethical individuality presented by the picture of the divine. In the words of one of the best recent discussions of the subject, 'Tragic drama...teaches us not that tragedy is unavoidable, but that it stems from confusing life with art'.[5] Tragedy is not about 'fate', about external forces acting on a helpless human subject, but about a moment of the self's *misrecognition* of itself as already unified and made open to true thinking in virtue of being identified (through conformity with a divine image) with embodied ethical value. The specifically tragic arises when the subject's conviction of being wholly identified with value in its obedience to this or that particular imperative leads an agent to deny or contest another subject's equally misrecognized self-identification.[6] Because this rests precisely on misrecognition on both sides, both sides are profoundly damaged: the world that is properly and adequately 'thought' is a world in which the subject recognizes itself in the other and is not competing with the other to define shared meanings. If, then, I treat the other's passionate embodiment of value as hostile to my own, I am indirectly undermining my own openness to the wholeness that is my destiny or vocation as a truly thinking agent. What I am denying is what I need for my own truthful self-presence.[7]

II

Thus the problem in the lethal confrontation between Creon and Antigone is not that they stand for genuinely different and incompatible values, not even that they hold their convictions with an unreasonable obstinacy, but that they are invested in their convictions in a way that denies or subverts the possibility of truthful thinking. In Hegel's terms, they see themselves as *aesthetic* objects, as sharing the static givenness of the images of the divine which they look to. They are caught in a particular stage of discovering self-awareness: the stage itself is inevitable, but the fatal collision is not. It depends on the extreme self-identification of a person with the heroic or divine image. In doing the right thing out of the desire to be at one with the imagined or projected divine, the subject runs the great risk of creating an opposition to another agent who acts similarly. For Hegel, when a subject learns to think, she is learning how to advance from misunderstanding to a more constructive misunderstanding, and at last to the rooted recognition of the other as subject in a way that makes the life or reality, the interiority, of the other something I need for my own self-recognition. I know who I am in the act of recognizing that I *am* only in the entire complex of relations with others, in the 'lawful' environment where there is no gap between what I legislate for myself and what my environment demands of me. So when a subject identifies with one particular value or imperative in such a way that it must be defended against others as if the survival of one value entailed the destruction or abandonment of others, the development of thinking and thus the development of spirit (free, self-legislating, communal human identity) is frustrated. The deadlock of rival values means literal and spiritual death.

Hegel is insistent on two points which are, for most readers, difficult to hold together. On the one hand, 'we must above all place on one side the false notion of *guilt* or *innocence*':[8] classical tragic narrative is not about flawed choices made by individuals who might or should have known better; it is about characters who in a significant sense do not *choose* at all. They enact who they are 'and never anything else'.

They are always both 'innocent' and 'guilty': they understand and accept the consequences of their actions, they do not look for absolution or even compassion, as if they knew their 'guilt'; yet they do not consciously decide on evil and so exhibit a sort of wholeness. As Hegel says in the *Phenomenology*, 'innocence is an attribute merely of the want of action, a state like the mere being of a stone, and one which is not true even of a child'.[9] Tragic agents do not seek to claim that they do not know what they were doing or that they are not responsible for their actions. And because they are identified with the value they see so compellingly and serve so unswervingly, the fact that this value is only a part of a greater whole must mean that their identification dooms them to death: their own human individuality is shattered in the collision with other embodied values because it is so bound up with the partial perspective whose partial nature is precisely what has to disappear. Thus in *Antigone*, Creon and Antigone are equally 'justified': each will maintain an unflinching commitment to what they believe is right because it is felt as a commitment to their own identity or integrity. Creon insists that Polynices has set himself at odds with the very idea of the city and the law. He has attacked Thebes with the intention of wrecking its holy places and overturning the laws of the gods (73.319–27),[10] so it cannot be that he is owed anything by the city, the law, or the divine powers. In one clear sense, *he does not exist*. The pretence that he does is a fundamental offence to law itself, and the ruler's responsibility is to uphold law at all costs (94.746–56). Creon elaborates with an argument that sounds, to a modern ear, like a piece of arbitrary patriarchalism: women must not triumph over men. If Antigone is left unpunished, 'I am not the man, not now; she is the man/ if this victory goes to her and she goes free' (83.541–2); and the defence of 'men who live by law' entails not allowing women to prevail (94.756–61). But Creon is not simply being a primitive sexist; the point is that he will cease to be what he is if a political decision —a decision about the limits of the law, about who counts as existing in a law-governed city—is going to be taken by a woman. The phrasing reinforces Hegel's point: Creon will not be a man if he fails to enforce his edict, his definition of the city's limits.

But Antigone is committed to two things which obstinately fail to fit into Creon's framework. The more obvious (and the more frequently discussed) is the obligation of *kinship*, which cannot be overruled by the city. The assumption seems to be that the common life of the city makes no sense without the concept of an absolutely *given* solidarity under the law of the gods which the fact of kinship embodies most plainly. Paradoxically, the act of honouring her kin brings 'glory' to her, the approbation of the city which recognizes this act of loyalty as a fundamental expression of obedience to divine law and so sees her death too as glorious (63.86–92, 64.112, 84.560–5; and cf. 95.775–82). It is not that Antigone is turning away from the idea that the city is the source of honour; her quarrel is with a ruler who sets the city's self-definition above the unchanging laws of the gods as expressed in family piety. Notoriously, she even says (105.995–1004) that she would not take the same risks for a child or a spouse as she would for her brother, as this is a unique and irreplaceable relationship: she can never have another brother, and so there is no possibility of making reparation, satisfying the specific debt owed to this particular kind of relationship. If she does not do her duty to Polynices, she will always be a failed sister—but she could have another child or husband and discharge her duties afresh. It is a sharp reminder that her sense of obligation is not to Polynices as an individual but to *a brother* as such.

The second aspect of her commitment, and a theme that runs through the whole text of the play—in sometimes disturbing ways—is that her action in disobedience to Creon is an act of fidelity specifically to the *dead*. 'I will lie with the one I love and loved by him—/ an outrage sacred to the gods! I have longer/ to please the dead than please the living here' (63.87–9). Ismene's refusal to help Antigone will bring 'the hatred of the dead' upon her (64.109). Death will be a gain to Antigone, as she is honouring the 'gods/ beneath the earth' (82.502) who are (paradoxically) alive forever. 'Death longs for the same rites for all', she tells Creon (85.584), who in turn mockingly urges her to 'Go down below and love,/ if love you must—love the dead!' (86.592–3), and accuses her of worshipping death (100.875–8). Antigone describes herself as having given herself to death 'long ago, so I might serve the dead' (88.631); she speaks—echoing Creon's scornful words to his son, Antigone's fiancé (93.728–30)—of 'wedding' the god of death (102.908) and looks forward to embracing 'the great growing family of our dead' where she will be welcome (105.981). The language weaves in and out between the idea of something like an act of incest with Polynices, the image of marriage with death itself, and the appeal to a universal human solidarity 'underwritten' by the fact of death. If Creon is preoccupied with the proper limits of the law (including who it excludes as well as who it protects), Antigone is preoccupied with the kindred we all ultimately belong to, the family of mortals, from whom no-one can be excluded. The unconditional solidarity and given-ness of ordinary kinship is not only an image of the law of the ideal community but an image of our ultimate and universal 'belonging' together in the realm of the dead. Creon's sarcastic 'love the dead!' is for Antigone a perfectly serious imperative; that is exactly what her rebellious and transgressive action is about.

What do we owe to other human beings? Creon and Antigone are both passionately committed to answering this question as clearly and decisively as possible. For Creon, we owe respect and the ritual acknowledgment of dignity to those who have not broken the basic contract of the human community; those who have profaned the holiness of the city and its shrines have no claim, and to pretend that they do is to strip actual citizens (and actual rulers, of course) of real and present human solidity and solidarity. A solidarity that includes those who refuse and undermine it is at best useless and at worst self-defeating; in any case, it is abstract. Citizens need a solidarity that is constituted by living persons in genuine mutual relation. For Antigone, we owe respect to any and all, because nothing is more universal than the death we all confront; nothing can justify human distinctions or exclusions in the face of the reality of death. The simple non-negotiable character of kinship relations—especially the specific case of the irreplaceable brother—is a reminder of what an unchosen, unconditional human bond looks and feels like. Creon may complain that Antigone's version of solidarity is empty; Antigone may claim in response that Creon's is no less open to the reproach of being self-defeating. If the sacred bond of the city is not grounded in the 'chthonic' realm—the realm of the gods under the earth, and the omnipresent sacred demand of the dead for respect—civic solidarity is arbitrary.

Hegel in his own discussion of this drama insists (rightly) that 'Creon is not in the wrong'.[11] He has a serious moral case—weakened, it must be admitted, by his personal petulance and by the suggestion that he is implicitly claiming to 'own' the city as its ruler (97.824–7). But Antigone's equally serious case is also weakened by her adamant refusal to engage with Creon's most weighty argument against her—that she is in effect preferring solidarity with the dead to solidarity with the living, when she is, in fact, as much in debt to the fabric of an ordered social world as anyone else. 'Her obedience to the royal prerogative is an obligation', says Hegel,[12] and what she is trying to do is in effect to *reduce* the substance of ethical obligation to the level of 'sentiment'.[13] To make decisions at the level of Antigone's absolutism about the family and universalism about the dead, 'the gods under the earth', is a refusal of ethical *action*, of the self-aware and transformative engagement with the acts of others which constitutes the embodied social practice to which the subject must in its matured condition turn. It is not a standoff between public and private or authority and conscience, though it has so regularly—and often fruitfully—been misread in this way. It is a collision over what we have seen in earlier chapters to be one of the fundamental themes of tragic drama, the question of what is owed to other persons. From the vantage point of Hegel's 'speculative' philosophy, the tracing of the mind's awareness of itself, Creon's problem is that he wants to absolve himself of obligation in a particular and extreme case; while Antigone's problem is that she treats obligation as having no specific content beyond the recognition of a general claim that is based on the universal fact of mortality. Neither is wrong in what they affirm: obligation to others has an ineradicably social form, and it is also not a matter in which we can decide to lay down limits. We do not 'own' the order of social solidarity so as to be able to alter its terms: this is why Creon is wrong as well as right, because he is claiming the freedom to limit the scope of human obligation, to make it conditional on civic solidarity. The prophet Tiresias expresses this starkly in his final protest to Creon, when he rebukes Creon for depriving the 'gods under the earth' of their right: he has no authority over the dead—and neither do the 'gods above' (115.1191–3). He has in effect forced the gods above, the guarantors of civic peace, to intrude beyond their sphere; he has made them unjust in this respect, and so stirred up a violence that will rebound on his own head. He has set the sacred in opposition to the sacred.

At the same time, we cannot properly reduce this solidarity to a *sentiment* of universal affirmation; which is why Antigone is also wrong as well as right, because she affirms a universal solidarity in death which ignores the actual continuing labour of making solidarity *work*, morally speaking, for living agents. The point is not made in exactly these terms, but she too is setting sacred against sacred, introducing violence into the world of holy obligation—though at least she does not, as does Creon, create an intrusion by one realm into another. What is tragic—and what, for Hegel, pushes us into a deeper 'speculative' framework—is the fatal identification by Creon and Antigone of their sense of individual meaningfulness and freedom with the discharge of the way they read their obligations. Creon and Antigone have made themselves fixed objects of self-contemplation. Their identity and value are as solid and externalized as the principles they uphold. But any self so contemplated is a *fiction*, since no self can be intelligible in this way as an atomized external object; and so they are profoundly at risk. As they pursue their fictions at the expense of any fuller awareness, they doom themselves to destruction—literally in the case of Antigone, morally and emotionally in the case of Creon. What they have failed to do is to find meaning and integrity in the shared enterprise of thinking, the unfolding of 'spirit' in mutual recognition and misrecognition—not in self-identification with an external ideal.

Hegel develops this argument further in his contrast between ancient and 'modern' tragedy. Classical tragedy belongs, as we have noted, with a certain stage of the discovery of the freedom and individuality of spirit, the stage in which our acceptance of a moral order (legislating for ourselves) takes the shape of identifying with a fixed external set of requirements. Tragic conflict occurs when different agents identify with different sets of requirements to the exclusion of all else. But with the dawn of modernity and the eventual advent of the romantic subject, there is a crucial shift of focus. The modern subject does not identify with an external imperative but with an individual and *internal* set of requirements. 'In modern romantic poetry…it is the individual passion, the satisfaction of which can only be relative to a wholly personal end, generally speaking the destiny of some particular person or character placed under exceptional circumstances, which forms the subject-matter of all importance.'[14] So, in contrast to the classical focus on what the gods and the city require, and on the passion to find identity in absorption into these requirements, modern tragedy is most fundamentally about what the individual requires to be *this* individual irrespective of any external imperative, 'The principle of the personal life in its independence has asserted its claim', says Hegel.[15] The tragic agent in modern drama may be a figure deliberately repudiating the gods and the city in one way or another, as in Schiller's *The Robbers*, where the figure of Karl Moor is taken by Hegel as illustrating the refusal of all collective and civic morality. But even where a protagonist does not simply deny all such constraints, the actual interest of the drama will be, for the modern writer and audience, in the way in which *individual* temperament, emotion, circumstance, and so on constrain action. Conflict is no longer essentially about externalized pressure, about a set of imperatives 'out there' with which the agent is driven to identify; it is about an ultimately self-contained model of integrity or authenticity. Modern tragedy may well be about conflicts that are played out in the public realm, in relation to public shared principles; but the point of the drama is to explore how inner and private 'wishes and necessities',[16] as well as sheer contingent events in an individual's life, work on the decisions made by the protagonist.

Hegel recognizes that Shakespeare's tragic drama supremely exemplifies what he is talking about. Dramas like *Macbeth* and *Othello* present us with eloquent, vital, realistic subjects driven not by conflicting and externalized ideals but by intensely particular passions. Internal conflict is now at least as significant as external (something which Hegel sees as foreshadowed in some classical drama, especially Euripides) in the sense that the suffering we witness is not simply a catastrophe worked out in the events overtaking the characters but an 'agon', a struggle, within the agent and in some instances a catastrophe in the soul, a crisis of authenticity. Creon and Antigone are bound to their commitments—to the city, to the universal community of the dead; the 'modern' hero, in Hegel's terms, may be torn between commitments, actual and possible, and the significance of those commitments is bound up with their role in securing personal integrity rather than just their intrinsic imperative quality. To take an example from a well-known twentieth-century drama: Robert Bolt's popular and vivid play of 1960 about Thomas More, *A Man for All Seasons*, has More explaining[17] to a baffled Duke of Norfolk why he will not compromise his loyalty to the authority of the Pope. 'What matters to me is not whether it's true or not but that I believe it to be true, or rather not that I *believe* it but that *I* believe it', says More. It is wholly implausible in the mouth of the historical More, or indeed practically any of his contemporaries, but it illustrates exactly Hegel's point: what is morally central is not the principle in itself but the way in which the holding of the principle becomes a test of sheerly individual integrity. The dramatic interest is not primarily in the conflict of clashing imperatives in the outside world but in whether More can sustain his personal moral position. Later on, More responds to his daughter's plea that he swear to the Act of Succession that will in effect legitimize Henry VIII's assumption of supreme authority over the Church with a powerful metaphor: 'When a man takes an oath, Meg, he's holding his own self in his hands. Like water. And if he opens his fingers then—he needn't hope to find himself again.'[18] More is driven by what Hegel would call 'the formal necessity of [his] personality'.[19]

We need to pause for a moment to clarify what all this does and does not have in common with what Hegel believes is going on in classical tragedy. Hegel's Antigone is of course allying her own survival as a moral subject with the defence of her commitment to a universal obligation towards the family of mortals. But she is not consciously *solving the problem* of personal integrity by adopting a specific set of principles. Within Hegel's overall philosophical structure, she has to be seen as developing the idea of an independent individuality by means of identification with the imperative she recognizes: she is taking the first steps to becoming a self by projecting individuality, self-legislating freedom, onto the gods who command her, and then identifying herself with the freedom and separateness of those gods. Bolt's Thomas More, on the other hand, *knows he is an independent self* already. As an independent self, he has elected to be loyal to certain principles, so that the betrayal of those principles is a betrayal of his primordial freedom and dignity as an individual. The tragic energy of Sophocles' drama lies in the inexorable conflict between visions of duty that neither of the main characters can possibly see as *chosen*. Creon does indeed go through a change of mind in the course of the play, faced with Tiresias's blunt charge that he has 'robbed the gods below the earth' and tried to extend his authority to the dead with whom he has 'no business' (115.1188, 1191). He has to give up what he has most set his heart on, the visible exacting of the city's justice against Antigone. But the drama does not linger over his internal struggles, and the dramatic point lies elsewhere; he is convicted of having both misrepresented and confused the nature of divine authority, the balance between earthly and heavenly sacredness (as we noted earlier). He is not wrestling with the question of how to sustain his individual moral integrity.

But there is a continuity between the classical and the modern in Hegel's scheme. The essence of the tragic in both is the self's misrecognition of itself. The pre-modern self seeks individuation and liberty through identification with an objectified divine order; the modern self seeks the same by trying to protect a pre-existing, 'given' integrity of the inner life. The pre-modern misrecognition results in a lethal collision between agents who have failed to understand that their ethical passions are not at odds with each other; the modern misrecognition results in the absolutizing of a given set of self-images, so that maintaining the self's integrity becomes a matter of terminal rivalry with the claims of other selves. Hegel's ideal moral situation— the state of 'lawfulness' in which what I legislate for myself is understood as identical with what all others legislate for themselves—requires every agent to identify the failures in thinking that lead to mythical pictures of a given and fixed selfhood and to reimagine the search for integrity or 'authenticity' as the search for mutual intelligibility and recognition,[20] with all that this implies in acknowledging my misrecognition or misconceiving of my own selfhood. For ancient and modern tragic narrative alike, the core of the conflict is to do with understanding the self 'aesthetically'—as an object for contemplation, either in virtue of its identity with authoritative and sacred schemata of behaviour or in virtue of its own primitively sacred character as a given, unique source of value. The heart of Shakespeare's genius, Hegel observes, is in his capacity to present characters who 'contemplate themselves objectively as a work of art', who are 'free artists of themselves',[21] just as the genius of the classical dramatists is to present characters who contemplate themselves—in a very specific sense—as 'gods', as embodiments of what is to be loved or served. In Hegel's view, Hamlet is supremely the artist of himself: his crisis is the question of how he is to be himself in a world of pervasive falsity. But the great figures of classical tragedy know (all too well) how to be themselves: they could not be at all if they did not in their own minds embody transcendent imperatives, as both Creon and Antigone do in Sophocles' masterpiece.

III

The continuity and disjunction between Sophocles' *Antigone* and Anouilh's—the most influential modern reworking of the story—would be material for a book in its own right, but it is worth noting briefly how Anouilh does very much what Hegel might have predicted he would in making the narrative contemporary. In the long confrontation with Creon, which forms the core of the play, Antigone's reply when Creon asks who she is doing this for is 'For nobody. For myself';[22] and later on, when Creon has almost succeeded in persuading her to forget her fantasies of heroic action and settle down in happiness with Haemon, she responds:

'What kind of happiness do you foresee for me? Paint me the picture of your happy Antigone. What are the unimportant little sins that I shall have to commit before I am allowed to sink my teeth into life and tear happiness from it? Tell me: to whom shall I have to lie?...All I want to know is what I have to do be happy...You tell me that life is so wonderful. I want to know what I have to do in order to be able to say that myself.'[23]

Like her classical predecessor, she chooses death, virtually insisting that Creon execute her; when he orders the guards to take her away, she cries, 'At last, Creon!'—with the stage direction indicating that she is 'relieved', *soulagée*.[24] This is an Antigone for whom what is at stake is the will never to lie or compromise; but we are in the dark as to what Antigone will or will not compromise *about* other than the will not to compromise. The value for which she dies, the ethical passion, in Hegelian terms, is her autonomy, an autonomy so absolute that it shrinks from the dependence and mutual negotiation that belong with human 'happiness'; and the inescapable conclusion for her is that she must die.

Those early audiences in wartime Paris who were confused by Anouilh's failure to offer them a clear drama of resistance to absolutism (specifically to the German occupation) had missed the crucial speech by the Chorus[25] in which the distinction is drawn between tragedy and melodrama (*drame*). Drama belongs in a world where death is terrible because it is avoidable, accidental; where it is worth struggling or hoping. 'The dear old father might so easily have been saved;

the honest young man might so easily have brought in the police five minutes earlier.' In contrast, tragedy is always already 'there', waiting to be activated, a sort of mechanism in which 'There is a sort of fellow-feeling among characters'. Tragedy is 'restful', *tranquille*, because there is no hope, so that all you can do is 'shout as loudly as you can': 'You can get all those things said that you never dare say.' Argument is pointless because, 'In tragedy, where there is no temptation to escape, argument is gratuitous: it's kingly.'[26] Passages like this are a significant warning to those who would read the play as it is still too often presented, as a *drame* about justified resistance to tyranny. What Anouilh offers in place of a morality play of this sort, with a heroine who risks everything for principle, is a deeply troubled reflection on the cost of decision and commitment: Creon maintains passionately in response to Antigone that someone has to take the burden of responsibility and guilt in public action; Antigone's protest comes close to arguing that any commitment involves a diminution of individual integrity. If we are to read the play against the background of the Nazi occupation, there is a good case for seeing *Creon* as standing for principled resistance, with the guilt entailed. But we probably ought to heed Anouilh's warning against any moralizing or edifying interpretations: tragedy is the release of a mechanism, so he affirms, the mechanism that swings into action when pure will is pitted against unyielding reality. Antigone is a clear example of Hegel's modern tragic protagonist, consistent, courageous, 'stable', someone whose actions and decisions develop from a single fundamental point in the self's conception of itself. Yet part of the tragic action is that, in the end, Anouilh's Antigone *does* find the prospect of death terrible and no longer knows what she is dying for;[27] and Creon has lost every prospect of 'happiness' in the performance of his moral duty to the city, as if he, as much as Antigone, is acting according to an abstract conception of who he *must* be rather than responding to what is imperatively before him. Both are confused modern selves at the end; neither can understand their commitment as a commitment to recognition, to the mutuality of law, and both are condemned to live and die in a schism between reality and integrity.

You could recast Hegel's thesis about the metaphysical significance of tragedy in terms of this schism. Tragedy tells you what happens when self and truth part company. It forces you (as Anouilh says) to speak what you have refused to know—that the self which is, whether in a classical or in a modern framework, a finished object to itself, a work of art, is precisely that: a *work of art*, a constructed thing, a fiction in the most literal sense. Hegel (unlike Plato) does not *quite* believe that metaphysical maturity ought to banish fiction,[28] but he insists that we *think* what fiction is doing, rather than simply carrying on with our self-constructions and taking them as given and independent realities. Fiction can simply indulge these myths, giving us endless constructed egos to fantasize about; it can be an elevated form of gossip and prurience. Tragedy is there to assist us in identifying the universal and unavoidable moments in the evolution of the conscious self when we *create* selves—whether in unexamined religious or moral contexts or in what we might call a primitive existentialist mode, in an assertion of the sacredness of a true and interior subjectivity. The projection of law on to external divine power in classical tragedy and the comparable projection on to an unassailable inner life in modernity are equally testimonies to the need of 'spirit' to claim a territory that is not purely about contests of power in society or about external models and behaviours imposed on the thinking agent. As such these projections are salutary and necessary moments. But the assertion of these projections as true, as unconditionally grounding the right and dignity of the individual, will lead to disaster. It is not possible to live on the basis of such a fiction. This is what we would rather not know; but this, as Anouilh puts it, is what we must now 'shout' or 'yell out', as more uninhibited translators have rendered it.

But tragedy is not—for Anouilh or anyone else—simply an inarticulate yell of unillusioned anguish. Relating this to the discussion in the last chapter, what this analysis implies is that 'thinking about suffering' is fundamental to thinking about thinking. To the extent that thinking about suffering, representing suffering in the complex and diverse means that tragic drama employs, obliges us to see both the dangers and the possibilities of our language, it makes us look harder at what awareness itself involves. We have seen that thinking about suffering—in the ways that a dramatist like Shakespeare makes us think—reveals both the way in which we can move on from seeing suffering as not communicable, not shareable (so that we can begin to develop language for compassion) and also the ways in which our language can encode strategies of managing, manipulating, magnifying, or diminishing the pain of others. In the light of this, we can see our language—and so our thinking—as always linked with a set of problems about power: mutual recognition is a radical unsettling of familiar power relations, because it requires my silence and my learning (my de-skilling, we could say, or 'unlearning', to borrow Thomas Hardy's word), not my defence of a stance or an advantage. To the extent that our language moves in this direction, it moves definitively towards the world of law, mutual acknowledgement, intelligent interdependence. And if this is true, tragedy exists to persuade us, repeatedly and diversely, to think better.

IV

And this immediately brings us to the question of that post-tragic 'reconciliation' which, as presented in Hegel's scheme, causes so much disquiet among certain commentators. Typical of such a reaction is the comment of Jennifer Wallace in her admirable *Cambridge Introduction to Tragedy*,[29] where she quotes from Hegel's discussion in his *Aesthetics* a passage about how the audience of tragedy finds 'satisfaction of the spirit' in accepting the 'necessity' of what has been enacted, 'and only then can our heart be morally at peace: shattered by the fate of the heroes but reconciled fundamentally.' She protests: '*Satisfied* when Antigone has hanged herself? *Morally at peace* when Creon, bereft of all his family, is hounded from the city into exile? We might, at this point, want to side with Aristotle and reply that human passions are unavoidable and intractable, not to be schooled out of us by the calm Hegelian voice of reason.' It is an intelligible reaction, but not, I would argue, a fair one. It is not, as Wallace maintains, that Hegel wants us to stop feeling sympathy with the characters and to move on to a calm apprehension of universal rationality. It is part of the encounter with tragic narrative that we are profoundly disturbed and forced out of our comfort zones; but the point of tragedy is not simply disturbance. In the wake of tragic drama, we are not only expected to feel something but to have learned something, to have discovered something about thinking. The language of 'satisfaction' and being 'morally at peace' is unappealing and misleading. Hegel is emphatically not proposing that the suffering of individuals should not move us or that we should concentrate on the majestically unrolling advance of 'reason'.

Read again his pages on the actual dramas, especially on Sophocles, and it is hard to believe that he meant words like 'satisfaction' to have the complacent Panglossian tone we may think we hear in them. The last thing Hegel is saying is that everything is all right really, that individual wreckage is smoothed over by universal benefit. We are 'satisfied' in the sense that we are not left with an assertion of utterly incompatible moral orders, a conflict between the gods above and the gods below, in the terms Sophocles uses. 'Necessity' does not mean that suffering is so mechanically inevitable that it no longer costs anything in real human lives. It is a way of underling the truth that certain kinds of misrecognition are bound to destroy human agents. And being 'morally at peace' is not about believing that the suffering witnessed is no longer troubling; it is about sustaining the conviction that what has happened is, precisely, outrageous, menacing, and yet at the same time capable of contemplation and of being represented in speech. This moral peace is the knowledge that the catastrophe of the tragic narrative is *not* an inevitable destiny but an episode in the discovery of thinking. In other words, Hegel is saying something very nearly the opposite of what some of his critics think he is saying: not that pain and suffering are less serious than you might imagine or that they deserve less particular and compassionate attention, but that their very seriousness and particularity test the capacity of thinking to breaking point. If we find that after all we can speak of these things (and obviously we do, otherwise we should not be discussing tragic narrative at all), the moral order has not disappeared; which means that we were right to think that what has happened is terrible and disruptive, even heart-breaking, but that we have come to see how this disruption has challenged and altered us, how it has made us know what we did not know or were refusing to know.

Returning to Martha Nussbaum's critique of Hegel, we may note that, especially as a reader of Sophocles, she sees Hegel as offering an intellectual project for the avoidance of conflict: 'The elimination of conflict is, for Hegel, both an acceptable and a plausible aim for a human ethical conception',[30] and so he does not see the tragic problem in terms of the urge to avoid moral conflict, only in terms of the one-sidedness of the visions of the protagonists. Nussbaum argues, very interestingly, that while speech is praised in the play as a miraculous creation of the human mind (as an aspect of law and civic intelligence),[31] it is precisely speech that traps both protagonists in their 'simplifications': no wonder that the dying Haemon stares in silence, like a wild animal.[32] Hegel, we are told, has too much faith in 'progress',[33] he is 'optimistic', even 'sanguine',[34] confident of a future that will rise above contradiction in triumphant rationality. But once again, it cannot be too strongly emphasized that Hegel is *not* arguing that 'reason' will overcome contradictions and produce triumphant order. Insofar as we can speak of a triumph of reason, it is our discovery of how deeply we have misunderstood what we are as spirit or mind; we now know what we must search out and change in ourselves. To say that Hegel seeks 'the elimination of conflict' can make him sound like a negotiator, working to establish a sustainable compromise between positions. But Hegel is in fact asking for our positions to be rethought from their foundations. He wants the very idea of a 'position' to be scrutinized. If the taking of a position is meant to be a case of commitment without moral risk, as both the classical and the 'modern' tragic agent are tempted to think, it ends in destruction. That is to say, if I seek to avoid moral risk either by identifying with transcendent authority or by appealing to a sacred and untouchable interior life, I am looking to take myself *outside* the realm of actual historical argument, error, penitence, and learning which constitutes the life of spirit; I want to stop (or not to start) thinking. The 'triumph' of thought is not the triumph of a comprehensive system of rational values but the emergence once and for all of a universal practice of mutual attention and exploratory speech—putting it boldly and question-beggingly, a practice of reasoning love.

Hegel himself clearly does not find it all that easy to state what he means by tragic reconciliation, and he again distinguishes between how this might work in ancient and in modern tragedy. Classical tragedy represents the vindication of 'eternal justice',[35] whose universality confronts and overcomes the partiality of the commitments of the protagonists. Modern tragedy requires something much more abstract and complex: we need to understand that the tragic conclusion, however immediately distressing, corresponds with something in the nature of the character. Thus Hamlet, says Hegel, is from the first oriented towards death in the excess of his spiritual and intellectual passion; and Romeo and Juliet do not have in themselves sufficient ground for their transcendent love to establish itself and grow. We recognize a sort of justice—not remotely in the sense of punishment for misdeeds but in the sense of an appropriateness in the character's fate to the nature of that character.[36] With other sorts of tragic protagonist—especially in the dramas of Schiller and Goethe, our 'reconciled' response comes from acknowledging the various ways in which their actions inevitably provoke forces that will destroy them: they act in such a way that they and we know things will end badly, but we and they can either take comfort from 'a more exalted and indestructible condition of blessedness' not realized in present history, or in the survival of a character with all its dignity intact even in the face of utter failure.

It must be admitted that these passages read awkwardly. Hegel's touch is far less sure in the discussion of modern drama, and the accounts of how reconciliation works in this context are unconvincing. However, the main line of argument does not depend on the detail of these readings. The central argument as it is made at length in the *Phenomenology* is simply that tragedy exhibits what happens when self and truth fall apart—in Hegel's language, when there is a 'severance between ethical purpose and actuality'.[37] Actuality, truth is to be found only in what is right—that is, in what is as it should or must be in the realm of spirit (which entails mutuality and so on). So if the world as it is crushes the individual agent, something must be adrift as between agent and reality, self and truth; my legislating for myself must be askew, and so the implication of the tragic outcome is that I must surrender what I thought was my selfhood and recognize that it has been shown to be less than real. Hegel's strained attempts to make sense of Hamlet or Romeo and Juliet are an effort to suggest how there is something in these characters that is imperfectly real; they are—to use his terminology elsewhere—aesthetic objects, beautifully crafted images which have to be dissolved in the face of actual constraint and decision. The more deeply a character is identified with the image, the more definitive is the destruction that awaits.

Whatever we say about this approach, it will not do to see it as a hymn to rational progress or an evasion of emotional involvement; Hegel grants that our emotional state, when faced with the conclusion of a tragedy like *Romeo and Juliet*, is an 'unhappy blessedness';[38] we recognize what is going on, we see the structure of the drama in relation to the emergence of thinking, but this does not make us cheerful or optimistic at the level of our feelings. If, as Gillian Rose argues,[39] Hegel's vision is indeed ultimately comic, we should not suppose this to mean that it is simply charged with positive emotion. To call it comic is to acknowledge that—as Houlgate also insists[40]—tragic conflict and the destruction of tragic protagonists is not the same as the representing of a world in which tragic suffering is unavoidable (which is why tragedy, for Hegel, must be nothing to do with 'fate'). Understanding why tragedy matters, for Hegel, is completely different from constructing a 'tragic world-view', whatever exactly we might mean by that. Hegel insists that tragedy represents a stage of the development of spirit, when we identify with either an external or an internal fixed image of the self; and, more specifically, it represents what can and will go wrong in this stage. This is not in any simple sense a stage in the history of culture that is somehow left behind, since we recapitulate spirit's history in our own thinking. Nor is it, even for an individual, a moment in an intellectual biography. It is a habit or skill of self-recognition which has to be integrated into mature interdependence, the recognition of self in the other towards which all human action and thought moves. What we cannot say is that existence is tragic: that would be tantamount to saying that there is no continuity in thought, and so no standpoint from which we can see and feel suffering for what it is. A fully tragic worldview, for Hegel, would be one that undermined its own position by removing the perspective from which we can see what it is for humans to live unreal, deluded, and profoundly pain-ridden lives. The comic side of Hegel's vision is the affirmation that there is nothing that cannot be looked at truthfully; this is very different from the idea—which some of his critics evidently ascribe to him—that there is nothing that cannot be looked at with moral, emotional, and imaginative equanimity. Thinking back again for a moment to the story of Akhmatova at the prison gates, it may be possible to see how truthful speaking about suffering might happen: neither a formless lament nor an emotionally sanitized fiction.

In this light, we can revisit Walter Davis's strictures on Hegel, discussed at the end of the last chapter. Davis complains that Hegel wants to reduce conflict to order, and so to deny the constructive energy of an ever deeper disruption of the self. Davis resists above all the idea that tragic art is a releasing of tension, since he sees this as necessarily diminishing the role of tragedy as offering access to buried levels of affect and injury. Yet Hegel's approach, I have argued, cannot be reduced to a consolatory happy ending or a dissolution of real conflict into consensus. To the extent that Hegelian interpretation always assumes that misrecognition is the driver of thought, we cannot treat Hegel as if he were assuming that we could attain a state of uninterrupted rational stability (as individuals or as a political and cultural community). Every construct of the self carries the possibility of misrecognition and so of tragic collision. What Davis provides, I believe, is a supplement rather than an alternative to Hegel's analysis. A Hegelian understanding of the tragic does not have to be a delivery from anguish; as we have seen, grief may still be present in the awareness of reconciliation. If the tragic imagination works solely in Davis's framework as the constant excavation of unresolved affective crises, it risks becoming a paralysing uncertainty, a *mise en abîme* of dissolution. If, as Davis wants it to, it opens up the possibility of a different kind of action, both *upon* the self and *by* the self, something of the Hegelian perspective will need to be invoked. What Davis sees as the formation of *psyche* is not all that far from a Hegelian formation of spirit: it is not the attainment of control by an emotionally measured, rationally stable individual subject, but the awareness of how deep-rooted the fictions of the self are in the human constitution.

V

So once again we are pointed to the connection between tragedy and knowledge. Experiencing the tragic through dramatic representation is a matter of experiencing the fragility and illusoriness of certain myths of selfhood—and thus also certain myths of civic and collective human life. The classical tragic protagonist is someone who does not yet know that she cannot arrive at self-consciousness by binding her identity to an external sacred order. The modern tragic protagonist equally does not know that she cannot arrive at self-consciousness by assuming a timeless ground of inner integrity and moral solidity, a 'true self'. Tragedy obliges us to think the actuality of pain and failure—which means thinking what generates pain and failure rather than lamenting its inevitability. Anouilh's Chorus, with their language about the 'gratuity' of tragedy and the mechanical way in which it moves into action, are not offering a theory about tragedy which depends on some model of unavoidable or universal pain; they are testifying to the way in which tragic narrative or drama represents the consequence of a confrontation with what we do not know; and what tragedy then does is to give us a voice to speak out what we now know—or at least what we know we don't know. It is 'gratuitous' in the sense that it solves no problems and offers no *theory* of reconciliation. The fact of the drama is intrinsic to the possibility of reconciled awareness—so that we cannot imagine that reconciled awareness means any analgesia, any easy calming of feeling. The 'calm of mind, all passion spent' of Milton's *Samson Agonistes* (a text we shall return to)[41] is a very limited and limiting reading of tragic reconciliation. But there is something important in acknowledging that the response to tragic narrative is not meant to be purely emotional.

Tragedy is a narrative of sad and terrible events. But what makes it more than a catalogue of such events, which are indisputably common enough, is the way in which the narrative seeks to exhibit the *sources* of particular kinds of error and suffering, not so as to soften the impact of the pain displayed, but to allow us to *see* the pain as it is absorbed, spoken, shared, not shared, used, made sense of, not made sense of; how it becomes a cultural experience. In so doing, if Hegel is right, tragedy aims to make us think not only about suffering but about thinking, about what the human subject characteristically does. And if Davis is right as well, what emerges is a new capacity for truthful or 'apt' action, action that is not dictated by an unreal picture of the ego. At the end of the first chapter, we noted that the discovery of our ability to narrate tragedy in the way that drama does brings us to the edges of the sacred by insisting that we attend to what disaster and pain do *not* take away from the human world, what bonds are *not* broken by failure and anguish. And this suggests that we need to think carefully about appeals to 'absolute tragedy', to a supposedly pure form of tragic narration that allows no excesses of meaning or presence. As we shall see in the next chapter, thinking about tragedy can be lured into this kind of essentialism; but how does this relate to those trends in modern drama which, whether or not we call them tragic in an exact sense, seek deliberately to explore the extreme and unrelieved representation of pain or degradation? Are such dramatic enterprises committed to a 'tragic world view' of the kind we have seen reason to suspect? Or can they still be accommodated within the discourse of tragedy? I believe there is a case for the latter, but it will need some careful mapping.

There is an obvious question about the relation of tragedy as we have been discussing it here to the 'theatre of cruelty' advocated by Artaud and developed by others such as Jerzy Grotowski and Peter Brook.[42] At first sight, the concern of a theatre of cruelty to engage with the subconscious, to shock an audience into pre-reflective reaction, has echoes in Davis's insistence on a theatre that intensifies rather than releasing tension. In a very telling phrase, Artaud claims that his concept of the theatrical event is intended to restore the 'agonising magic relationship to reality and danger' that is abandoned or 'prostituted' in conventional theatre.[43] Theatre has to get beyond 'magic' and engage an audience in cosmic or 'metaphysical' encounter, creating in its working the kind of violently critical moments that trigger metaphysical epiphanies—'temptations, vacuums' around the great metaphysical insights to do with creation and chaos.[44] This entails the kind of assault on an audience's sensibilities that Artaud associates with oriental (Balinese or Japanese) drama, a theatrical idiom in which ordinary language is left behind. Theatre must open up 'a deeper, subtler state of perception',[45] and this is induced by unexpected sounds, spectacle, physical rhythm, visual shock, visual stylization (including the use of masks and puppets), combining in a 'hieroglyphic' style.[46] Artaud's programme for his theatre includes not only re-stagings or adaptations of Shakespeare in a way that reflects contemporary cultural fragmentation (Charles Marowitz was to work this out further), but also dramatic representations of mystical Jewish texts about the violent energy of spiritual challenge and transformation, dramatizations of the Marquis de Sade's texts, to bring out the interfusion of cruelty and the erotic (realized famously in the *Marat/Sade* of Peter Weiss), and Elizabethan plays 'stripped of the lines', that is, reduced to schematic representation of plot and character.[47] It is important to see that Artaud is not simply arguing—though he is sometimes misrepresented in these terms—that the staging of extreme cruelty is essential to authentic theatre: the cruelty is directed towards the audience as well as enacted on the stage. Or rather, the *extremity* of both the matter and the medium of the drama is what gives it its authority. His vision is of a theatre that allows the audience no space to escape into, a theatre that makes a radical and comprehensive claim. As Davis puts it—in one of his rather surprisingly rare allusions to Artaud—the goal is to produce an image whose 'violence allows no inner distance', where the awareness of the image is coterminous with the knowledge that things must change, the subject must change, must be born again.

In this sense, Artaud's agenda has something in common with Hegel's: a proper understanding—or, better, reception—of tragic drama is a moment in the evolution of the subject, and without it we remain hidden from ourselves. What Artaud and Davis are emphasizing is that this uncovering of the subject is something that happens precisely in *crisis*, in the recognition not of a moral truth in the abstract but of the traumatic factors that force us habitually to deny what is necessary for our life, for life which is not paralysed by denial and safe self-images. Hegel would have been, to say the least, startled by Artaud's passionate appeal for a restoration of the primordial shock tactics of extreme sound and spectacle; but he might have allowed that this rediscovery of a kind of 'liturgy' was not as completely alien as it might superficially seem to his own project of thinking tragic drama as a necessary way of thinking about thinking. 'Theatre', says Artaud, 'is a crisis resolved by either death or cure'.[48] We might think back to Nussbaum's formulation of 'healing without cure'[49] as one of the things that tragic drama seeks; but what Artaud means by 'cure' is, I think, something other than a way of ending, pensioning off, the recognition of suffering (which is what Nussbaum is justifiably nervous of). Whatever terminology we settle for here, the important thing is that tragedy is seen as a therapy; and that to see it in this light is not to see it as any less cruel, any less an assault on surface complacencies. It is essential to recognize that the satisfaction or justification or reconciliation which is for Hegel the moral effect of tragedy is not a perception or emotion felt by a sensibility that has surfaced unchanged from the trauma of pain and failure that is represented on the stage. The subject that acknowledges reconciliation is one that has been radically altered in and through the dramatic transaction. What Artaud is drawing attention to is the actual method of alteration. On the far side of it, the subject is not the subject we started with (or as): we are not returned to a place of safety, the ego is not offered a comfortable place to be. The mutual recognition, the journey towards law and compassion that is figured in the tragic experience requires a disruption that will leave our habitual perceiving and feeling seriously wounded; incurably wounded, the tragic narrator hopes, knowing that this is the only kind of cure that addresses the depth of our trauma and dysfunction as individuals and societies and begins to reconstitute us as *psyche*. It may well be that Hegel's rhetoric of 'moral peace' to characterize this new condition is uncomfortably static or enclosed in its resonances for contemporary readers; but I have argued that it needs to be read carefully against the background of his scheme in its completeness. Davis's insistence on trauma and the disturbance of our habitual and destructive ways of handling trauma begs fewer questions, it seems; but we should at least do Hegel the justice of trying to see how his version of tragic knowledge as reconciliation is not wholly different in kind from Artaud's kill-or-cure language.

Perhaps we could take an example from fiction rather than drama to focus this a bit more clearly. A. S. Byatt's rich and challenging sequence of novels, beginning with *The Virgin in the Garden* in 1978,[50] follows (among other narrative lines) the experience of a priest, Daniel Orton, who has to confront not only an appalling bereavement but estrangement from most of those he loves most deeply. He is a difficult and complex figure, not always sympathetic; but it is clear as the four novels unfold that he attains the status of something like a moral point of reference. He is not reconciled to his suffering or to the God who is supposed to make sense of it. To that extent, it would be odd to ascribe anything like 'moral peace' to him. But he inhabits his loss, his isolation, and his commitment to routine, small-scale human care, with a measure of honesty and fidelity that gives him an unusual, unmistakeable authority. He is not cured; he is not forgetful; he is not paralysed. His trauma has left him permanently wounded, but at the same time grounded in a selfhood that is basically not afraid. He is a character who fleshes out the point at which Davis and Hegel might converge, a character both could recognize as confirming something of their analyses of post-tragic growth or transformation. Both would say that what we know or know afresh on the far side of encounter with tragic drama is that the knowing self we began with must disappear and be reconstituted. Both see this reconstitution as the gateway to metaphysical imagining—thinking what would need to be true of our total moral environment to make possible and intelligible a way of inhabiting the world like Daniel's.

Notes

1. *Hegel: Lectures on the Philosophy of Religion. One-Volume edition. The Lectures of 1827*, edited and introduced by Peter Hodgson, Berkeley CA and London, University of California Press 1988, especially pp.352–7.

2. *Hegel on Tragedy*, edited and introduced by Ann and Henry Paolucci, Westport CT and London, Greenwood Press 1978 (second edition), p.74. Although this relies on older translations, frequently from texts that cause modern editors a good many problems, it is still the most accessible and convenient collection of texts for English speakers, given that improved modern editions have not all found translators—and that many earlier discussions have relied upon these versions of Hegel's lectures.

3. References as translated by Robert Fagles, *Sophocles: The Three Theban Plays*, Harmondsworth, Penguin Classics 1984 (revised).

4. *Lectures on the Philosophy of Religion*, pp.343–6, 350–2 on the religion of beauty.

5. Stephen Houlgate, 'Hegel's Theory of Tragedy', in Stephen Houlgate (ed.), *Hegel and the Arts*, Evanston IL, Northwestern University Press 2007, pp.146–78, quotation from p.146; this very comprehensive and lucid essay is much the best survey of Hegel's thinking on the subject in the current literature in English and makes full use of improved and more recent editing of Hegel.

6. Ibid., p.149 (referring to Hegel's discussion in his lectures on aesthetics).

7. Ibid., p.150.

8. *Hegel on Tragedy*, p.70 (the text is from Osmaston's translation of Hotho's edition of Hegel's lectures on the philosophy of art, a composite text).

9. Ibid., p.278.

10. References to Fagles' translation.

11. *Lectures on the Philosophy of Religion*, p.353.

12. *Hegel on Tragedy*, p.73.

13. *Lectures on the Philosophy of Religion*, p.353.

14. *Hegel on Tragedy*, p.60.

15. Ibid., p.81.

16. Ibid., p.84.

17. Robert Bolt, *A Man For All Seasons*, London, Samuel French 1960, Act 2, sc.1, p.49.

18. Ibid., Act 2, sc.7, p.76.

19. *Hegel on Tragedy*, p.88.

20. Once again, cf. Gillian Rose, at p.44 above.

21. *Hegel on Tragedy*, p.86.

22. Jean Anouilh, *Antigone*, translated by Lewis Galantiere, *Jean Anouilh: The Collected Plays*, London, Methuen 1967, p.211.

23. Ibid., p.220–1.

24. Ibid., p.224. The sense of Antigone's *Enfin, Créon!* here is almost 'You've finally got it!'.

25. Ibid., pp.201–2.

26. Ibid., p.202. The printed text actually has 'kindly', a misprint. The original is: *Dans le drame, on se débat parce qu'on espère de sortir. C'est ignoble, c'est utilitaire. Là c'est gratuit. C'est pour les rois.* ('In melodramas you can argue because you hope to find a way out. It's all utilitarian, not very impressive. But with tragedy it's all gratuitous. By appointment to royalty.').

27. Ibid., p.230.

28. Hegel believed that 'art' as a category was something necessarily surpassed by mature dialectical thinking; but this does not mean that he thought art was now impossible or improper. See Stephen Houlgate's Introduction to *Hegel and the Arts*, especially pp.xxii–xxiv, and the essays in this collection by Martin Donougho and J. M. Bernstein.

29. Jennifer Wallace, *The Cambridge Introduction to Tragedy*, Cambridge University Press 2007, p.124.

30. Martha Nussbaum, *The Fragility of Goodness: Luck and Ethics in Greek Tragedy and Philosophy*, Cambridge University Press 1986, p.67.

31. The reference is to 77.395ff. in the play.

32. Nussbaum, *The Fragility of Goodness*, p.75.

33. Ibid., p.77.

34. Ibid., p.78.

35. *Hegel on Tragedy*, p.89.

36. Ibid., pp.90–1.

37. Ibid., p.280.

38. Ibid., p.91.

39. See especially Gillian Rose, *Mourning Becomes the Law: Philosophy and Representation*, Cambridge University Press 1996, chapter 3, 'The comedy of Hegel and the *Trauerspiel* of modern philosophy', pp.63–76.

40. Houlgate, 'Hegel's Theory of Tragedy', p.146.

41. See pp.127–9 below.

42. Antonin Artaud, *The Theatre and Its Double*, London, Calder and Boyars 1970; Jerzy Grotowski, *Towards a Poor Theatre*, New York, Simon and Schuster 1968; Peter Brook, *The Empty Space*, London, Penguin 1968.

43. Artaud, *The Theatre and Its Double*, p.68.

44. Ibid., p.69.

45. Ibid., p.70.

46. Ibid., pp.72–3.

47. Ibid., pp.77–8.

48. Ibid., p.22.

49. Nussbaum, *The Fragility of Goodness*.

50. A. S. Byatt, *The Virgin in the Garden*, 1978, *Still Life*, 1996, *Babel Tower*, 1996, and *A Whistling Woman*, 2002, all London, Chatto and Windus.

4

Absolute Tragedy and Moral Extremity

I

Metaphysical imagining can take more than one shape, and one of its more provocative forms is the idea of '*absolute* tragedy', as developed most eloquently and challengingly by George Steiner. For Steiner, it is one key aspect of a wider cultural polemic. In his classic essay on *The Death of Tragedy*, he argues that Europe after Rousseau had, broadly speaking, lost the capacity to construct genuinely tragic drama or narrative. This is due to three connected cultural developments. First: once the prevailing account of human agency has made room for the idea that human suffering and disaster are radically detached from human responsibility, the tragic hero becomes unimaginable. The weight of responsibility carried by a classical protagonist must appear as a kind of category mistake in the modern ethical world; adjusting the environment will adjust the scale of human risk, so that there are, for modernity, no dilemmas that are in principle incapable of resolution.[1] Second: classical tragedy assumes a cosmic order with which humanity cannot negotiate, an order represented in shared myth, ritual, and image. In the absence of such a sacred canopy, tragedy cannot be a corporate experience but will slip towards melodrama, the depiction of an individual's contingent struggles against 'fate' or something similar.[2] And third: the language used in modernity is incapable of carrying the weight appropriate to tragedy; our words, like everything else in our culture, are commodified and stale, mere operations of an efficient but jaded intellect. We do not know how to speak seriously in a culture that is so wedded to exchange and negotiation, to the 'market' in one sense or another; we have no vocabulary for what we cannot negotiate with, and without such a vocabulary the tragic imagination atrophies.

It is a complex argument, and—in the nature of the case—an impressionistic one, connected in Steiner's overall work with, for example, his controversial assertions about the role of major political trauma and social injustice in the generation of great literary works, and his concern for the reaffirmation of 'presence' as a necessary category in the interpretation of texts, over against what he sees as the postmodern absorption in textual surface and interpretative liberty.[3] But, leaving on one side the complexities of these wider issues, his point about tragedy is one that needs some careful parsing. It is not simply that he is writing off contemporary experience as somehow unworthy of being dignified with the name of tragedy—though his rhetoric gives hostages to fortune on this and allows some credibility to those who charge him with a restriction of the category of the tragic to an elite. He is *not* saying that modern suffering is not interesting enough to be called tragic; he *is* saying that our representation of suffering has become 'thinner'. The tragic is to do with the 'homelessness' of humanity in the universe—rooted in a primordial alienation between humanity and cosmos, a falling out of grace.[4] If we have no doctrine of what it might be to live *in* grace, no sense of an order that we have made inaccessible to ourselves, there is no irremediable loss and so no tragic vision. Thus, in relation to Steiner's points about the modern 'imaginary' listed above, the tragic requires a recognition that human agency has upset the order of things. Reducing our suffering to the level of environmental malfunction offers us a drastically different perspective, in which human intelligence can modify the environment to its needs rather than being driven to the end of its resource or crushed by an inexorable other. The way in which humanity has upset the cosmos may or may not be a matter of what we would see as moral culpability, but (as in the case of Oedipus) it is a human act that lies at the root of the crisis, not a set of impersonal pressures. The demythologized modern subject is one that cannot be imagined as locked in irresoluble conflict with a wholly given (and largely inaccessible or unknowable) sacred cosmology: the idea of 'fate' (and Hegel too was scathing about the lazy way in which such a notion was deployed in thinking about tragedy[5]) is a pale reflection of this primitive vision, amounting to little more than the way in which a contingent fall of circumstances happens to make trouble for a protagonist—issuing in melodrama rather than tragedy.[6] As we have seen, Anouilh would have agreed (though Steiner allows what Anouilh does not, in giving 'trivial' circumstance a place in tragedy, and can evoke just the wistful contingency Anouilh deplores and sees as typical of melodrama—'had the messenger reached Cordelia's executioners half a minute earlier...'[7]). Finally, in a world stripped of the sacred, meanings are always going to be disposable and exchangeable, never crushingly difficult, because presence has evaporated; and so there will be no words for what we are *bound* to wrestle with.

'Without the logic of estrangement from life, of man's ontological fall from grace, there can be no authentic "tragedy".'[8] And Steiner, revisiting his early arguments, gives them a further twist in more recent essays by insisting on a 'core of dynamic negativity' in authentic tragedy, resisting any 'contamination by hope'.[9] It is in this spirit that he is prepared to see even *Lear* as an 'impure' example of tragedy (as opposed to *Timon of Athens*, which specifically calls for language to end).[10] In all this, he is building on a cumulative unease with 'modern' tragedy that is rooted in Hegel's conclusion that modern or romantic tragedy cannot have the same function as classical Greek drama in simply embodying a moment of spirit's self-recognition, because other vehicles for this (theological and philosophical) are now available. It is reflected also in Kierkegaard's *Either/Or*, where the impossibility of a modern tragic hero is seen as a result of the lack of any non-negotiable moral frame of reference. Kierkegaard, in apparent sharp contrast to Steiner, argues that this 'modern' assumption leaves the human agent wholly and unequivocally responsible for her acts—rather than being (as Steiner wants to argue) given over to a discourse about how external agencies shape human decision and possibility: although being wholly responsible in this way is, for Kierkegaard, tantamount to not being 'responsible' at all in the ordinary sense—beyond both pity and blame, locked in the project of unqualified self-creation. But Steiner goes a good deal further than any of his predecessors in seeing the essentially tragic imagination as positing a real metaphysical duality between guilty humanity and an 'innocent' or indifferent cosmos, whose diverse powers 'lie in ambush' for us.[11] Thus, 'The summit of tragedy in English literature is Faustus's intuition, via Marlowe's speculative and philosophical genius, that a deity

capable of forgiving Faustus would be a false god.'[12] Tragedy is always
played out in the eye of a god, even if that god is absent, infinitely
receding, hostile, or indifferent; that is to say, tragedy posits a transcendent order, a myth of perfect or reconciled existence—a place from
which humans are forever exiled, or a state of being to which humans
can never in any way attain.[13] The whole point of tragedy is that no
god can bring about a reconciliation between humanity and the cosmos; no god can make us at home, no god can make us god. Steiner
may echo Hegel in some respects, but here he parts most decisively
from him in insisting that the ultimate 'recognition' that takes place in
tragedy is the acknowledgement of a self-inflicted and terminal rupture with the world. It is not just that there is—to use the phrase we
used earlier[14]—a gap between self and truth which has caused deep
damage and has to be addressed. The gap must be at the deepest
level unbridgeable. Returning to his comment on Marlowe's Faustus,
Steiner seems to be saying that a god who would resolve the schism
between humanity and the cosmos would have to be a god capable of
betraying his identity with the innocent or unknowing or indifferent
cosmos, betraying *himself* by allowing the possibility that humans could
be at one (atoned) with him. A true god can only respond to the atrocities of human pain as does Dionysos in Euripides' *Bacchae*: Zeus
has ordained and there can be no more questions. Or, as Dionysos
announces at the beginning of the play, the point is to prove that he
is indeed a god, and *therefore* indifferent to the chaos and horror
he causes.

Steiner lists some of the other classical dramas which he regards as
authentically tragic, including *Antigone* and Aeschylus's *Seven against
Thebes*, as well as *Medea* and *Trojan Women*. All represent the divine as
refusing to justify itself, refusing to respond with either justice or mercy
to human cries of anguish and protest. It is a powerfully consistent
reading as far as it goes; but—in the light of the perspective we have
taken so far in this book—it leaves some large and troubling questions.
The most important is that the 'absolute' tragedy that Steiner wants
to identify is essentially a *text* rather than the kind of shared event we
have been considering in this study so far. What I have been calling
tragic narration or representation is a process of enactment that seeks
to involve a community—whether the strongly liturgical community
of ancient Athens or the more transient community of the modern

(post-mediaeval) audience. It seeks to invite, lure, or startle them into thinking afresh about their processes of thought and self-representation, political as well as personal. Even some of the classical examples Steiner offers of the 'absolute' genre, as we have seen in the case of *Medea* and *Antigone*, construct specific questions about the failures and dilemmas of the city and the mechanisms of corporate blame and expulsion; they are not purely opportunities to contemplate moral extremity. As public utterance, they imply public reception and response, not a fixed metaphysical conclusion about humanity in the cosmos. To read them as stating a final, cosmic deficit in reconciliation is to reduce them radically as *drama*. Steiner quotes several times the 'not to be born is best' dictum which Sophocles puts into the mouths of the Chorus in *Oedipus at Colonus* (though it goes back before Sophocles' time) as illustrating the consistent dualist vision for which he argues; yet it is risky to suppose that this phrase, deployed consciously as a familiar axiom by the Sophoclean Chorus, represents a simple final judgement on what is most significant in the drama; it is a moment of emotional hopelessness which has to be heard alongside and within the entire discourse of a drama which is undeniably unsparing in its delineation of abjection and pain, but not a long statement of despair. The telling phrase about 'the contamination of hope' should make us uncomfortable: the quest for pure and definitive literary form is always shadowed by the passion to *ignore* something in the actual material work. And if tragedy is itself importantly about helping us *not* to ignore, it would be strange if the paradigm of tragic purity should require us not to see or hear what is actually being represented.

And part of what is being represented, in ancient and modern tragedy alike, is, as I have argued already, a perception of suffering as capable of being spoken about. A strictly Steinerian tragedy, we might say, is compromised as soon as it opens its mouth, because it is committed to representation, and so to an undetermined future exchange of words. It can be argued about; the very act of putting on the stage a narrative that defies explanation and consolation as rigorously as Steiner's strongest examples do, invites debate. We are properly silenced by the extremity we witness, but emerge with possibilities of speaking differently; and, as we have noted, that transition may be drastic enough to merit being thought of as a 'new birth' of some sort.

Kathleen Sands puts it well when she observes that talking about the tragic is not seeking to define a *quality* of experience (very sad, disproportionately painful, and so on) but a *mode of narrating experience*: 'To define tragedy...is to discern what makes suffering good to tell.'[15] Even a Steiner would have to offer some thesis as to why the unrelieved darkness of the absolutely tragic narrative is 'good to tell', why creative effort is devoted to its articulation, and why people actively want to witness it. And even the admission that in 'absolutely' tragic narrative we recognize a condition that belongs to us *as humans*, not concedes something to the specific set of humans whose troubles are being told.

Then there is the difficult issue of what tragedy says about the divine or the sacred. Steinerian tragedy directs our attention to at least three perceptions of the gods: that they are actively malevolent, that they are beyond our questioning, and that they are incapable of rectifying what is amiss in the world or between the world and the human spirit.[16] But these perceptions are in fact seriously different from each other, and equally hard to map onto the actual language of tragic drama. If the human agent in tragedy is struggling against an alien *will*, the tenor of the drama is profoundly altered: the tragic protagonist is the victim of another—a rival and contingent—agent, and this pushes the drama further towards *melodrama*, a narrative that traces the conflict of egos and implicitly seeks our pity for the victim of active injustice. It is parallel to the pitiable story we tell about someone struggling with fate; both the 'fate' story and the 'battle with malevolent powers' story distract our attention from what Steiner wants to be the heart of tragic narration—the primordial human act that opens up the wound in things. If the gods are beyond questioning, never justifying what they do, that leaves open whether our response is to be awed acceptance, as often in the words of the classical Chorus, or despairing revolt. If the gods are incapable of resolving any of the human world's tangles, what is the status of their presence or intervention? It is true that Dionysos in the *Bacchae* is an unapologetically destructive presence; but as he says, he is out to establish that he is indeed a god and that therefore he deserves more from Pentheus than he gets. If he is not given his due, chaos results for the city (through the destruction of its king); if he is acknowledged, his chaotic presence can be incorporated into the city's awareness of itself.

Steiner is also arguing something more complex about the role of the sacred, though. For a narrative to be tragic, it must be set against a 'hinterland' of shared meaning and expectation. Even if that hinterland is to some extent secular, even atheistic, it furnishes the necessary non-negotiable and non-explicable environment which is the necessary oppositional pole to the action and suffering of a tragic protagonist. Intriguingly, Steiner regards Büchner's *Woyzeck* as illustrating this point. It is, he says, a play in which the God-question is completely silent (this is true only with a good deal of qualification, as overt and not-so-overt biblical allusions abound[17]); all we have is a universal 'suffocation' and blankness, a moral vacuum of alarming intensity. But it is precisely this consistently (non-contingently) amoral environment that makes the play so effectively tragic, in Steiner's judgement: Woyzeck himself, the vulnerable and rather simple-minded soldier haunted by hallucinations as well as harassed by his social 'superiors', is relentlessly stripped of dignity and agency by a completely impregnable and indifferent system of authority, medical and military, that leaves him no capacity for agency except in the killing of his lover, Marie. The sheer intensity of the anti-humanist frame of *Woyzeck* provides a sort of 'mythos'. It is a world very deliberately shrunk to the proportions of agents instrumentalizing one another with no second thoughts; 'virtue' is the preserve of those who have social power. What matters is that this world, consciously drained of moral depth, has something of the same non-negotiable character as the sacred canopy of older societies: the very absence of the sacred is so insistently presented that it becomes a sort of reversed image of the traditional moral universe, 'a potent negative theology itself metaphoric of the tragic'.[18] I take the phrase 'metaphoric of the tragic' to mean something like this: Woyzeck is confronted with an 'order', represented by the doctor and his military superior, completely oblivious to his humanity; the drastically 'secular' attitude of these other characters to him—their refusal to allow him any interior life, any psychological presence—is an image of the complete moral otherness of the cosmic system in regard to human beings in classical tragedy. What is non-negotiably 'divine' in *Woyzeck* is the secular instrumentalism of the characters who possess power. But Woyzeck is not deprived of agency entirely; what is left for him is destruction and self-destruction, both an affirmation of a kind of freedom and a confirmation of the basic moral schism in the universe.

This is a quite problematic reading of Büchner's drama (complicated of course by the fragmentary nature of the text and our uncertainty about the ordering of the scenes), but it sketches the way in which Steiner attempts to preserve the possibility of some sort of tragic imagination in a Godless world. But his conclusion is that the only real equivalent in the modern age for what tragedy once sought to do would be a dramatic voice closer to *Woyzeck* than to Sophocles or Shakespeare, closest of all, perhaps, to Beckett.[19] The expression of a vision of absolute tragedy cannot any longer be tragedy as a literary form; contemplating a humanity essentially and eternally alienated from the universe it inhabits now imposes an absurdist idiom, since our world does not even *know* that it is Godless and has no vocabulary for expressing its Godlessness. When we have forgotten even what it is that we no longer believe, we cannot summon up even the negative image, the 'metaphoric' recovery of the tragic. Tragedy dies, and absurdism, 'black farce', is all that is left to us, so that our need is not for more books about tragedy but for a new theory of comedy, 'of the riddles of grief, singular to man, in the merriment of *Twelfth Night* or the finales of Mozart's *Cosi fan tutte*'.[20]

II

But *is* this all that is left? Recent theatre might suggest otherwise (and might also suggest that to describe modern reappropriations of classical drama as 'loans from the museum'[21] does them a lot less than justice). I have already mentioned the theatre of extremity developed in Britain by writers such as Edward Bond and Sarah Kane (the latter, interestingly, quite explicit about her debt to *Woyzeck*); and we need to look in more detail at what they attempt to see if they offer any counter-case to Steiner in terms of how a deliberately 'drained' moral world may generate a dramatic style that stands in continuity with the tragic—and to see also if these monumentally unconsoled dramas qualify other aspects of Steiner's case and reinforce the doubts expressed about the category of the absolutely tragic. Both Bond and Kane achieved notoriety in British theatre for their use of grotesquely extreme on-stage violence—including rape, mutilation, dismemberment, and cannibalism—and this reputation has led to a somewhat hazy focus in the discussion of their stature as dramatists. Jennifer Wallace quotes[22] a generally sympathetic critic's comment that Kane's 1995 play *Blasted* 'makes you feel but it doesn't make you think'. And if that were a fair verdict, Kane's drama would fail to be tragic in the sense we have generally used the word in discussion so far. But it is not at all clear that it is a fair comment. Certainly the play assaults the audience's sensibilities without let-up, a *Titus Andronicus* for the nineties, and there is an issue about how much assault an audience can manage before defensive de-sensitizing sets in; developments in Kane's later dramas suggest that she had taken the point. But it is misleading to say that the play does not make an audience think, and think in ways that echo the thinking that classical tragedy demands.

Blasted begins with two scenes involving Ian, a journalist, and an inarticulate young girl, Cate; these scenes depict what at first seems a familiar set of tropes about sexual exploitation and male insensitivity, but also insinuate with increasing force an edge of uncanny and disproportionate violence barely beneath the surface of the words and interactions. Ian at one point phones in to his newspaper a story—in flat journalese—about the murder of a young woman; he tells Cate that he has had a lung removed and may be dying; he plays with a loaded gun; he talks vaguely about people who might be after him for revenge and hints that he has done 'things' in the course of secret operations. His language is consistently abusive and extreme, a compendium of savage bigotries about non-Europeans, people with disabilities, women, even football fans. At the same time, he repeatedly turns to Cate for access to 'another place' which is not defined by the violence of speech and act that is Ian's imaginative world;[23] we have seen Cate having an unexplained fit,[24] a kind of prophetic or clairvoyant trance, and there is a hint that the 'other place' is something to do with the state she enters—a state which is like death, she says, and is both appalling and enviable in Ian's eyes. The arrival of the Soldier at the end of Scene Two—one of the more memorable *coups de théâtre* of the contemporary stage—is, at one level, the dramatic externalizing of the suppressed inhumanity and savagery of the preceding exchanges. We don't know whether Ian's allusions to covert operations, even his description of the surgery that removed his lung, are fantasy or fact; but the Soldier's irruption onto the scene brings the physicality of death and extreme pain further in to the play's world. Ian, humiliated and raped by the Soldier, is left with no words—the stage directions three times insist on his silence ('*Ian's face registers pain but he is silent*'; '*Tries to answer; he can't*'; '*Doesn't answer*')[25]—and the scene ends with the most graphic horror yet, as the Soldier sucks out Ian's eyes.

Between this and the beginning of the next scene, the Soldier has killed himself. This last scene of the play is set against a background of universal horror and grief—'everyone in town is crying', says Cate,[26] who has somewhere found an abandoned and dying baby. Ian attempts to kill himself with the now empty gun, in a farcical moment that echoes Gloucester's ludicrous attempted suicide in *Lear*, then is left by Cate who goes in search of food. Cold and starving, he eats some of the baby's corpse. Cate returns with food, obviously obtained ('There is blood seeping from between her legs') by selling sex to a violent man. Rain is falling through the roof of the now ruined hotel room where the action has been set, and the play ends with Cate feeding the dying Ian and his words—after silence and rain falling—'Thank you'.

Some reactions to the play have failed to see how the superficial naturalism of the opening scenes is not only rapidly dissolved but undermined almost from the start; there are all kinds of warning signs that this will not be another play about 'relationships'. Kane's later dramas are more explicit about how the extreme violence is to be staged/imagined; but even here, it should be clear that both time and place are pushed out of shape more and more in a way that dictates a non-naturalistic representation of physical extremity. The later scenes of *Blasted* involve the literal blowing apart of the hotel bedroom, a startling compression of the change of the seasons (from the hot summer weather of Scene Two to the freezing winter rain of Scene Four), and a very consciously indeterminate passage of time (hours? days?) when Ian is left alone in silence on stage after Cate disappears to find food. The universal devastation of the final scene ('everyone in town is crying') is hardly something that can have developed overnight. What were thought to be distant conflicts have literally erupted into the cramped emotional space of the opening and the single night in which Ian has forced sex onto Cate has become an entire shared or public history of terror and abuse. 'The final image of the play is arguably tender', says Jennifer Wallace;[27] but it is not this ending alone

that qualifies any judgement that the play is primarily a nihilistic catalogue of shocks. To go back to the categories used in thinking about
tragic drama in earlier chapters, we should note a number of resonances. Perhaps most obviously, this is *risk-laden* representation of suffering: its graphic quality deliberately challenges conventional barriers
of experience—both within the drama (the invasion of a domestic
scene by the signals and symptoms of major public catastrophe) and
between characters and audience, by refusing to work with an unspo-
ken convention of taste or restraint. And if risk-laden, then yes, not
always successful, genuinely risky; the play, like *Phaedra's Love* and
Cleansed, hovers on the edge of being absurd, unstageable, over-insist-
ent, disgusting and no more. Its aim, though, is not to offer a series of
gratuitous shocks, but to expose the interpersonal world in which it
begins as a paper-thin cover for the savagery that surrounds and pervades. So, far from making us feel rather than think, the drama pushes
us to attend closely to the grotesque self-characterization of Ian in the
early scenes. He is in the business of representing violence and pain,
at a number of different levels. As a journalist, he manages it through
glib and formulaic (and salacious) reportage; as a physical subject he
manages it through a blustering aggressiveness towards his own body
and its needs and towards any other bodies in the vicinity. He lives in
a milieu of low-to-medium-level violence, verbal, imaginative, and
physical, but the register and pitch of his voice tell us that he believes
violence is a 'style' he can manage, something of whose representation he can be in control. The arrival of the Soldier is a 'Dionysian'
moment: the uncontrollable asserts itself in the most dramatically
physical ways possible, in extreme threat and violation. Before the
rape and mutilation, but after he has poured out a series of stories
about atrocities, the Soldier challenges Ian: 'You should be telling
people'.[28] 'Tell them you saw me', he pleads[29]—and the pleading is
significant: Ian is in the business of telling, and only someone who
knows how to *tell* can deliver the Soldier from a world in which uncontrolled atrocity is everywhere and is nowhere present to anyone,
nowhere thought or pictured truthfully. The Soldier is condemned to
a kind of non-being. But Ian responds that his readers aren't interested in a story that isn't 'personal': 'Why bring you to light?' he asks,
in a very revealing turn of phrase.[30] The rape follows, the Soldier
'crying his heart out'.[31] At least one of the themes highlighted in this

exchange is another of the issues we have been considering: refusals to know. Ian speaks for a culture that is engaged in denying its own violence—not in the trivial sense that 'we are all guilty' in respect of global suffering, or that our immediate environment is morally nastier than we acknowledge, but in the sense that we refuse to represent to ourselves the hinterland of utter destructiveness lying within our habitual exchanges (hence the growing, edgy unsettlement in the opening scenes, the feeling of something just on the brink of horror). We do violence to ourselves by silencing our knowledge of ourselves; and so we leave the denied violence in a self-contained and wholly uncontrollable world of its own ('At home I'm clean. Like it never happened', says the Soldier[32]). Ian's inability to answer the Soldier after his rape tells us that the refusal to represent the extremity of destructiveness leaves us helpless in the face of it. Our clichés about violence, our titillating and trivializing versions of it, bring on the real and unimagined thing, and, like Anouilh's tragic characters, we 'yell' when we see what we had denied or ignored. And that is why Kane does what she does in intensifying the levels of horror so prodigally, as if challenging the audience: 'Domesticate this if you can!'

We noted earlier,[33] in discussing aspects of classical tragic representation, that 'To *avoid* confronting the worst atrocity is to make the self and the city less secure.' Silence about these things allows us to *be* silenced in our response, to accept tacitly that some things cannot be spoken and thus cannot be thought. And if violence cannot be thought, the self is left eternally divided, with its nightmares dominating one side of its life, without reflection or learning. Kane's drama could be read as illustrating Walter Davis's fierce prescriptions for tragedy—the exposure of what can't be borne in the 'crypt' of the psyche; but also the bringing to light of what can sustain the dissolving of all that serves the image of an ego at one with itself.[34] Cate's presence in the last scene, her inarticulate prayers for the dead baby over whose body she erects a cross, the provision of food through humiliation, terror, and death (the baby's corpse, Cate's prostitution for food)—all these fragments fill out just a little what Ian might have meant earlier by saying that Cate took him to 'another place'. The horrors of the action overall are not the only place for the human imagination, and relics of a 'eucharistic' vision (the sacred body sacrificed and broken for food) haunt the text. Similarly, in a later play,

Cleansed, where the violence is in some ways even more extreme but at
the same time more surreal, schematic, and ritualized, there is a profoundly moving leitmotif of *substitution*, pain accepted in or for an
other, as a vehicle for keeping love alive. One character, who has
offered to be killed in place of his lover, dies saying, 'It can't be this'.[35]
And the figure of Grace, whose passionate incestuous love for her
dead brother Graham has been a major theme throughout, is left
at the end, after a bizarre sex-change operation, 'transformed' into
Graham: 'Always be here' is one of her last lines, indicating that her
excruciating torment and humiliation has resurrected him, or at least
given him an enduring life. 'It can't be this' is what is drawn out of us
when extremities of violence are represented. We need to see and
know atrocity before we can see and know that it is not fated or
doomed for us; and in this sense, Kane is echoing the Hegelian insight
that tragedy is radically different from stories about struggling with
fate. So hers is a tragic narrative to the extent that it expects the self to
be remade in the process of witnessing and absorbing; without the
extremity of represented atrocity, we do not and cannot see why
the moral world we inhabit is not the only one. We are condemned to
the 'fate' of enacting the unthought; condemned to the divided world
of self-serving and trivializing representation (Ian's journalism) on the
one hand and the nightmare of mindless cruelty on the other. Kane's
dramas are advocating reconciliation in the sense that they refuse to
accept this duality, and, like Hegel, understand reconciliation not as a
happy ending or a tidy moral message emerging from chaos, but as
the possibility of contemplating, thinking, the whole of the psyche's
life, not only the superficially manageable parts of it; which finally means,
yet again, the imperative of *recognition*, finding that self-awareness
and the awareness of the other's awareness and 'investment' in awareness intersect and interweave—as, in the horrendous surgery of *Cleansed*,
the forced exchange of sexual identities is also a movement into a
radical compassion.

Kane's last work before her suicide in 1999 was a poetic mono-
logue, *4.48 Psychosis*, referring to the hour when she would regularly
wake during a time of acute depression, with a sense of utter lucidity.
'I had a night in which everything was revealed to me. How can I
speak again?'[36] Among the harrowing aphoristic lines of this unique
piece, we find: 'Body and soul can never be married',[37] 'They will love

me for that which destroys me',[38] 'I dread the loss of her I've never touched',[39] 'Don't switch off my mind by attempting to straighten me out',[40] and, at the very end, 'It is myself I have never met, whose face is pasted on the underside of my mind...please open the curtains'.[41] The text enacts as radical a dysphoria as Steiner could wish, but it also enacts an intensity of *desire* ('Validate me/ Witness me/ See me/ Love me'[42]). Everything is revealed; and so, strictly, there is nothing to say, because the plea to be seen (like the Soldier's desperate plea in *Blasted*) is always going to be denied and met with lies and consolation or 'explanation'. But surely something is said, something is *mourned* and so is thought? It is possible to long for the curtains to be opened and for me to meet myself—to be in some way at one with my thinking. Yet: every way of imagining that (including a reconciled erotic love) is untruthful, and once that is acknowledged there is nothing to hope for, no state of mind or state of affairs that will truthfully hold desire and clarity together. Yet again: denying desire is a violence of its own kind.

Kane's work, which in Britain still struggles, on the whole, to find the critical seriousness of response it merits, has features that make it at first sight a credible illustration of some of George Steiner's arguments; but it will not finally fit into that framework. Even more than *Woyzeck*, it addresses the atrocity of 'unthought' power (physical, political, medical, intellectual, sexual). Her reworking of the Phaedra story (*Phaedra's Love*) introduces the theme of how public narratives of sexual transgression both reflect individual sexual surfeit and boredom and also *deflect* attention from issues of power and manipulation. And the connecting of tragedy with the facts of human power, not with some general conflict with the universe, moves us away from the exquisitely unrelieved blackness of 'absolute tragedy'. 'It can't be this' and 'You take me to another place' are political as well as personal moments, recognizing that the order of atrocity and brutal oppression is not fated and natural, even if it is not escapable either. Hence the importance of the word 'mourning': pain can be lamented, perhaps even lamented in a way that transforms something in the viewing or hearing subject. As I argued earlier, Kane's surreal extremism of violence is about insisting on what cannot be domesticated but has to be acknowledged. It is not a voyeuristic elaboration of pain; it is interesting that stage directions give little indication of what the victims of the most extreme atrocity are meant to show in terms of physical feeling, and the not infrequent directions for uncontrolled weeping are not triggered by physical pain. And it is not an invitation to empathy in any conventional sense—indeed, much of the text could be read as discouraging a simply empathic response. Far more important for Kane than imagining what people in extreme physical agony might be feeling in their bodies are two distinct further questions—what characters are feeling *about themselves* (the Soldier's anguish that he is not and cannot be 'brought to light'), and what it is that finally drives characters to voice the desires that have been buried. So Kane's audience is not being invited to a potentially pornographic imagining of terror and suffering, but to a recognition of the scale of human breakage through our illiteracy about power and cruelty and the deep human separations they entail. The dismemberment of characters on the stage—at its most extreme in *Cleansed*—is a metaphor for that inner dismembering of the settled aestheticized self which tragedy sets out to dissolve: rather like the tantric Buddhist meditative disciplines that tell you to envisage being dismembered and consumed, so as to disaggregate the fictional finished self and allow enlightened and compassionate awareness to be born. It is perhaps an unexpected analogy for what Kane is doing, but a necessary reminder of her own clear commitment to that liturgical element of tragic theatre which we have seen to be so central.

III

Steiner's theses about absolute tragedy are not sustainable in the light of how the relevant tragic texts and performances work, and this brief excursion into the imagination of one contemporary dramatist has given reason to qualify any judgement that the tragic form is exhausted. But what Steiner does is to raise—in a way that cannot be ignored— the question of what it is that makes tragedy difficult or impossible; what are the anti-tragic impulses in human culture. At the centre of his argument is one particular characterization of the modern imagination which constitutes it, in Steiner's eyes, as essentially anti-tragic; and that is the assumption that there is nothing—no order of being, no divine impenetrability, no inbuilt human perversity—that we just have to come to terms with; nothing that cannot be negotiated, reworked, resolved by human resourcefulness. Steiner is surely right in insisting that tragedy as we have received it deals with aspects of human interaction and agency where conscious choice and control are conditioned or frustrated by what cannot be controlled—inherited patterns of revenge, hidden guilt, Dionysiac irruption, unarguable obligation; these presences in and around our acting and thinking selves cause suffering that could not have been predicted and conflict that cannot be resolved. They do not—and here I disagree with Steiner—add up to a metaphysic of radical or permanent human estrangement, but they do locate human agents in the middle of a vortex of forces that cannot simply be mastered by human reason and skill. To recognize this is not to accept a fatalistic view of the impotence of all human activity in the face of unchangeable laws mandating suffering or failure (hence the importance of Hegel's insistence that we are not talking about a struggle between freedom and 'fate'); it is a matter of seeing clearly that we do not have the secure purchase on our environment that would come (so we imagine) from a complete transparency about our own motivations, or a complete predictive clarity about the processes of the world we inhabit. To underline the point that has regularly recurred in these pages, tragedy is about the effect upon us of what we do not know.

This is why *accidental* misfortune cannot be the central stuff of tragedy, any more than 'fate' can. The fact that there is not time for Edmund's message to reach Cordelia's jailers is not what makes the end of *Lear* appalling: circumstance, character, a whole complex of interwoven lines of plotting lead to a moment in which the natural but shocking outcome of all that has gone before is displayed, and it is that whole complex that is tragic. Anouilh was right: to focus on the 'if only' sensation of sad contingency reduces this to melodrama (which is why, say, Hardy's novels, relying heavily as they do on 'hostile' circumstance as the trigger of catastrophe, remain melodramatic rather than tragic, with the arguable exception of parts of *Jude the Obscure*). Narratives of accidental misfortune are not trivial, and of course they also have to do with what we don't or can't know. It is fair enough to be told that accident is always possible and that there are no guarantees of an absolutely risk-free life. Our vulnerability as figured in such a context is real; but it is not radical in the sense that tragic drama wants to insist, not a matter of unmanageable forces inside and out. Suffering as a result of accident may be a *warning* to us to be more careful or less recklessly confident in our routine transactions; but what sense exactly could we make of seeing *Medea* or *Othello* or *Woyzeck* as fundamentally a warning against being careless? What a drama of accident cannot deliver is the recognition of my and our incurable vulnerability in respect of what we systematically fail to see in ourselves and cannot know about our world. Contingency alone is indifferently comic and tragic, depending on the effect of the accident; it is another sort of vulnerability, the ordinary uncertainty of life. And to say that ordinary uncertainty, even when it results in what we would habitually call 'tragic' consequences, is not the same as tragic narrative is not to make light of any kind of human suffering; as we have already seen, it is simply to say that telling such a story is not the same as strictly tragic representation. It goes beyond the reminder that we never know what's round the corner and should be cautious about assuming we do. The threat of what we don't know is deeper and more destructive of our habitual images of self and world.

One of the most significant ripostes to Steiner's case for the anti-tragic nature of modernity was Raymond Williams's celebrated essay on *Modern Tragedy*, with its strong protests against any elegiac looking back to tragic narratives of the fall of the great, any assumption that the paradigm tragedy is, as Aristotle would have claimed, to do with catastrophe overtaking the powerful or celebrated.[43] The commonplace complaint that 'tragic' is over-used as an adjective in modern language cuts little ice with Williams, who insists that the great shared experiences of disaster in the twentieth century, war, genocide, major population displacement, mass poverty and so on, are emphatically material for tragedy. But this entails, for him, a model of tragedy that is in important ways 'secularized'. We do not need a sacred canopy in the background; only the basic fact of historically conditioned conflict, a situation in which hope is denied and humanity stifled. Tragedy works by enacting the collision between existing order and imagined order—which is why it has revolutionary potential. For Williams, revolution is 'the inevitable working through of a deep and tragic disorder':[44] and his use here of 'tragic' directs us to the central importance for his interpretation of tragedy of the idea of loss for the sake of redemption. Tragic action is the acceptance of present loss, suffering, or compromise, in the light of the imagined order of universal equity, a society's 'incorporation of all its people *as whole human beings*'.[45]

We have been misled by the traditional assumption that tragedy always entails death and that individual death is what makes a drama tragic. But not all tragedy historically involves the death of a hero; and in any case, individual death is not the unmitigated catastrophe that bourgeois modernity takes it to be. If we focus simply on universal mortality and on the specific loss involved in the mortality of a 'tragic hero', we miss the point of the tragic narration, which takes us beyond individual mortality towards the recognition that death has many meanings, and that one of the meanings which can be constructed is of death as a moment in the creation of new order: 'I die but we do not die'.[46] Thus tragic drama presents, first, the specific staging of an historical context in which conflict is present, conflict between an order that denies wholeness to human beings and the human agents who are suffering under it; second, the process by which resistance to that order develops, including the ways in which this resistance generates its own new forms of alienation or suffering;[47] third, the climactic events by which, despite the tragic cost, some sort of humanist redemption is affirmed and the existing order is shown to be deniable, for all its capacity to kill or suppress.

Williams's Marxist convictions are clearly in evidence in this lucid and in many ways profoundly humane analysis; but they illustrate exactly some of the things that worried Steiner. At the root of the problem is the effective reduction of tragic experience to states of social conflict. Throughout the present book, we have seen reason to resist any analysis of tragedy that ignores its reference to the city, its consistent interweaving of the disruptions of soul and society; but this does not add up to a conclusion that all 'tragic' suffering must be rooted in identifiable kinds of social disorder. What, classically, disrupts the soul and what disrupts the city are intimately connected, but in a way that precludes any attempt to say that one is 'really' the other. Once the tragic has been redefined in these terms, as the effect of identifiable political malfunction, we lose the dimension of tragedy that is about the interconnected disruption of both our self-construct and our social and communal identities. Williams's characterization of the imagined order as one which includes 'all its people' has ample resonance with themes we have traced in earlier chapters—to do with the dangerous mechanisms of exclusion—but, in the context of his general argument, it raises problems of its own. If what is tragic is the way in which 'revolutionary' action throws up new forms of exclusion—if it means death to some of the agents involved—it leaves quite unresolved the basic issues of power in the situation: who has the power to decide what 'counts' as a meaningful death in this framework? If this question is ignored, then (as Walter Stein argues in a careful and sympathetic critique of Williams), the slippage from 'I die but we do not die' to '*you* die but we do not die' is dangerously easy.[48] Paradoxically, the systematic politicization of tragic crisis or conflict in Williams's interpretation creates a politically dangerous vacuum.

The implication of Williams's argument is that there is no single 'canopy' of meaning against which tragedy can be viewed; there are crises of inhumanity from age to age, each of which is formally tragic in that it involves social inequity and the conflict flowing from it, and displays the human cost of resistance. But, in this framework, to say that there is an ongoing, non-negotiable aspect to human tragedy would be to weaken the possibility of commitment to transformative action, to essentialize suffering, to forget the endless diversity of human pain or injustice; recognizing that diversity helps us to see that we do not have to deal with a single abiding problem, and so to see that revolutionary protest is intelligible, case by case. The difficulty with this, though, is rather as Steiner suggests: human suffering is the result of 'maladjustment' that is in principle curable; and this simply bypasses most of what traditional tragic representation struggles with. Williams's tragic vision does not allow for the kind of difficulty that changes the very terms of self-understanding; and to allow for such difficulty is not to commend some sort of fatalism—although Steiner's preoccupation with absolute tragedy skirts such territory—but to grasp that it is in recognizing the *shared* gravity (shared across time and circumstance) of the pain and disaster which arises from our failure to know ourselves and our world that we are ourselves reconstructed as agents or subjects.

In sum: the possibility of modern tragedy can be asserted, against Steiner; but Williams's assertion of it is equally damaging to a full understanding of what tragic representation has been and can be. But the one area where Steiner and Williams might coincide in their judgement would be in relation to what Steiner has to say about commodified language. A culture in which all signs are exchangeable, or in which no sign has a value that cannot be renegotiated, is one in which the idea of inescapable *cost* will not make sense. For Steiner, it is typical of contemporary speech that it seeks to cut loose its ties with 'presence', with depths of connection and significance that are inescapable for us; and although he would have plenty of questions about the link, it is hard to deny the parallel with the Marxian characterization of the capitalist universe as one in which nothing is fixed or stable, everything is caught up in the *danse macabre* of universal exchange. And the Marxist Williams is clear that tragic narrative is about just the inescapable cost that Steiner identifies: the imagined (possibly future) order for whose sake Williams's tragic agents suffer and fail in the present *is what it is* no less exigently than a Steinerian sacred canopy, and what is lost in the tragic struggle is genuinely and irreplaceably lost. A language in which values and meanings were entirely fluid would be inimical to tragedy because it would treat loss as an invitation to compensation, not as an invitation to mourning. The self imagined in such a world would be a self whose needs were capable of being catalogued and managed, not a self in process of formation by the dissolving of images and the awakening of buried trauma: an *unthought* self. Steiner's deepest question about the possibility of modern tragedy is a question about the modern self—isolated, articulate about its rights, wants, and projects, capable of marshalling and calculating its desires, compensating for the lack of this by the acquisition of that, seeking always an equilibrium of satisfaction for the moment. Is this straightforwardly the self that contemporary imagination must work from? So that—as Steiner hints—the future of any representation of the tragic has to be in the form of farce? It would be a useful exercise to look at—for example—the recent BBC drama series *Black Mirror* as a candidate for the representation of tragic material in satirical, often near-farcical, form: technology's ravaging of the map of human awareness, the confusion between the real and the virtual, media manipulation of our emotional lives, and the effect of this on moral discernment, private and public. These are sophisticated fictions which would bear on many of Steiner's concerns. But this chapter has argued that something more like the classical theatrical model still shows signs of vigour in work like Sarah Kane's. These dramas do more than develop 'thought experiments': they do the fundamental tragic work of de-familarizing, breaking down boundaries between private/interpersonal and public/political, forcing a re-thinking of what thinking might be.

IV

And one feature of these dramas is that they continue to allude to
specifically religious themes and vocabularies. Kane's Christian background—predictably and eloquently rejected in some of the texts—is
put to work in a variety of ways, in the poignant exchanges about
prayer at the end of *Blasted*,[49] in the use of scriptural cadence and
echo in *4.48 Psychosis*, in the argument between Hippolytus and the
Priest in *Phaedra's Love*.[50] This last, with its sharply focused alternatives
of forgiveness and death (self-forgiveness or self-chosen death), fore-
shadows *4.48 Psychosis* in suggesting that 'If truth is your absolute you
will die'[51]—which might seem to converge with Steiner's metaphysic.
But what differentiates it is the continuing dramatization of the underlying set of dilemmas: atrocity must be spoken, 'brought to light';
bringing it to light, representing it in the drama, displays the unfor-
giveability of both world and self; if forgiveness is not possible, the
alternative is death. This is not the same as talking about the homelessness of guilty humanity in an innocent/indifferent cosmos, nor
does it assume that a God who forgives conspicuous sinners (Faustus)
could not be God. Rather, it is a statement that death and absolution
stand in a precarious balance: an echo, but a significantly changed
echo, of Artaud's 'death or cure'. To show the reality of tragic violence is to articulate a plea for absolution, even if only the odd kind of
absolution that comes from being 'brought to light'. There is a need
for something to be told; truth-telling about atrocity is the condition
of some sort of affirmation of, even restoration of, humanness. Yet the
more truth is told the more remote the absolution seems. One way of
reading the cry in *4.48 Psychosis*, 'Fuck you God for making me love a
person who does not exist',[52] is as a protest against the possibility of
love in a world without absolution—the 'person who does not exist'
being the buried self, the longed-for affirming and witnessing other,
and, presumably, God. The tragic issue is not an indifferent God or a
hostile cosmos but the intolerability of a self emerging into 'light',
aware that the burial of the self is one kind of death and the 'coming
to light' of the self is another. What God could propose an absolution
adequate to the truth of the human world? But how can our language
silence the reality that signs of absolution and hopes for absolution are
part of our discourse and are no less insistent in demanding to be

spoken? Something undeniable makes us love; something undeniable makes us recognize that, to paraphrase Eliot, after some sorts of knowledge there is no forgiveness. The tragic imagination lives between those two 'somethings'.

Kane, then, reinforces Steiner's picture at least to this extent: tragedy is a deeply un-secular matter. A radically secularized imagination (and I shall come back to what exactly that might mean) would conclude that the 'somethings' just mentioned could only be conditioned moments in our self-construction rather than moments of coming up against the completely intractable. As with Steiner himself, this affirmation of the non-secular is not the same as the demand for a confessional agenda in drama. If tragedies need to be set against a background of clear religious faith, this would assimilate tragedy—in the way Walter Benjamin classically discussed in his *Origin of German Tragic Drama*[53]—to *Trauerspiel*, the drama of conscientious dilemma, martyrdom, death that illustrates a point of conviction, or a catastrophic crisis in political life where the monarch's power overreaches itself in tyranny (on this basis, *A Man For All Seasons* could rightly be characterized as a *Trauerspiel*). *Trauerspiel* is drama that narrates suffering or catastrophe firmly in the context of a moral calculus, and its goal is to affirm the vindication of true conviction. 'The martyr-drama was born from the death of Socrates as a parody of tragedy.'[54] Fully confessional drama is not trivial or dull (Benjamin succeeds in making that case), but it does not set out with tragedy's agenda of disruption and disclosure. Tragedy may or may not be written or realized by people who have clear religious conviction; what matters is that the action of the drama presents a world in which there is an unbridgeable gap between what human agents intend and control and what actually happens, internally and externally. The tragic agent is in touch with more than he or she understands. Turn this into a drama of conscientious resistance or (as with Raymond Williams) unavoidable social conflict and the result is less than tragic. Both confessional or edifying drama and the drama of revolutionary conflict as Williams describes it will end up doing less work on the forming of the *psyche*; worse, they may obstruct that process to the extent that they reinforce *positions* which the drama's action is meant to vindicate.

So the secular in this context means a version of narrative—whether novelistic or dramatic—in which agents are presented as *coinciding with their self-understanding*, coinciding with their ideals or self-images. Confronted with a 'secular' narrative in this rather specialized sense, if we were ever inclined to leap to our feet and warn a character on stage of what they cannot see, it would not be something about their own image and discourse but simply an accident or surprise waiting to happen (*Behind you!*). Or, to borrow language I have used elsewhere, it is to fail to allow a character (or object or situation) to have a dimension of life that faces away from me as knower or observer; to deny that what I see is seen by radically other and inaccessible eyes. Religious belief takes this for granted: what I see is seen by God and as such is seen in a way quite other to the way I see; in that otherness lies the freedom of what I see, freedom from my aims and capacities, the dimension that prompts patience and receptivity in my looking. And the residue of such a perspective is what saves any poetics from secularism, even if it does not mandate conventional belief.

We shall be moving on next to a longer consideration of tragedy and religious language. What this chapter has attempted to show is that the continually stimulating and provoking typology of tragic drama that George Steiner sketches makes it clear that the tragic imagination is in trouble in a society for which the unknown-ness of something or someone is simply a question of contingent lack of information. This does not commit us to a policy of static mystification; but it imposes the recognition that unfinished business is intrinsic to the specifically human act of speaking together.[55] That difficulty is thus a central aspect of our mental life and our language is a corollary of this; and tragic representation addresses the most abiding kinds of difficulty, the difficulties that surround our self-understanding as visible agents committed to shared meaning through speech and social activity. Tragedy tells us, among other things, that the roots of our difficulties lie at the roots of our very sense of selfhood, so that the disruptive narrative that reopens the path to primitive levels of trauma and fear is a necessary part of how we live in and with difficulty, and how we tell ourselves the truth. None of this commits us to the apocalyptic judgement that tragedy has become impossible in late modernity. If it is as necessary a form as all this suggests, it will find a voice, however untraditional, whether in black comedy or in—as I have argued—the risky extremism of a Sarah Kane. And again, resisting Steiner's pessimism about modern tragedy does not commit us to endorsing Raymond Williams's optimism about tragedy reconstituted as revolutionary threnody, a registering of the cost of necessary resistance. The signs are that it is still possible, even in a world of commodified language, half-thought-out voluntarism and widespread confusion about the limits of what human skill and decision can achieve, to create dramatic representations of the metaphysical terror and disruption that classical tragedy works with—and even representations of the imagined other place where an integrated, if not consoled, story can be told.

'Integrated, if not consoled'; the assumption that religious conviction is essentially at odds with tragedy, that tragedy is a fundamentally sceptical genre, rests largely on the belief that religion is bound to give a consolatory version of any narrative of suffering, and that this is a way of de-realizing the specificity of pain. At best, religious faith can give us one or another version of *Trauerspiel*, at worst a toolbox for denial. Yet if tragedy is obstinately non-secular in the sense that has been argued here, what exactly is it in religious discourse and story that does *not* simply generate illusory peace or acceptance?

Notes

1. George Steiner, *The Death of Tragedy*, London, Faber 1963, p.133.
2. Ibid., pp.292ff.
3. See, classically and controversially, George Steiner's *Real Presences*, London, Faber 1989.
4. George Steiner, '"Tragedy" Reconsidered', in Rita Felski (ed.), *Rethinking Tragedy*, Baltimore MD, Johns Hopkins University Press 2008, pp.29–44, quotation from p.30.
5. See, for example, *Hegel on Tragedy*, edited and introduced by Ann and Henry Paolucci, Westport CT and London, Greenwood Press 1978 (second edition), pp.71, 325: appealing to 'fate' is a refusal to see tragedy as a crisis for thinking. Tragic crisis is generated from within the world of thought—not from a supposed tension between the subject and the world of impersonal forces.
6. Steiner, '"Tragedy", Reconsidered', p.33.
7. Ibid.; cf. pp.66–7 above.
8. Steiner, '"Tragedy", Reconsidered', p.32.
9. Ibid.
10. Ibid., p.41.
11. Ibid., p.33.
12. Ibid.
13. George Steiner, *No Passion Spent: Essays 1978–1996*, London, Faber 1996, p.140.
14. See p.73 above.

15. Kathleen M. Sands, 'Tragedy, Theology, and Feminism in the Time After Time', Felski, *Rethinking Tragedy*, pp.82–103, quotation from p.83.

16. Cf. Steiner, 'Absolute Tragedy', *No Passion Spent*, pp.136–40; '"Tragedy", Reconsidered', pp.33, 35–6.

17. Steiner, '"Tragedy", Reconsidered', p.36 on *Woyzeck*: 'It transpires in a world of which God, if ever He was, is unaware. There is not…the intimation of a *deus absconditus*, of the "God-abandoned".' But for biblical and theological echoes in the play, see the apocalyptic imagery quoted in Scene Two (Georg Büchner, *Woyzeck*, translated by John Mackendrick, London, Methuen Drama 1979, p.5), the ironic hymnlike song at the opening of Scene Three (p.6), Woyzeck's reference to 'Suffer the little children to come unto me' in Scene Five (pp.11–12), the Doctor's mocking and scabrous allusion to David and Bathsheba (Scene Eight, p.1), Woyzeck's agonized appeal to God to 'blow the sun out' and the First Journeyman's pseudo-biblical rhetoric in Scene Twelve (p.25), Marie's allusions to the woman taken in adultery and the sinful woman anointing Jesus's feet in Scene Eighteen (pp.29–30), and Woyzeck's memory of the devotional text on the picture which his mother kept in her Bible (Scene Nineteen, p.30). Whether or not this is a world of which God is unaware, it is not a world unaware of God, and it is the fractured memory of a God-inhabited world that sharpens our perception of the massive, insane inhumanity of the powerful in the play. It is hard to see how this could be read as deliberate turning away from the vision of a 'God-abandoned' world rather than an emptily secular one.

18. Steiner, '"Tragedy", Reconsidered', p.36.

19. Ibid., p.44.

20. Ibid.

21. Ibid.

22. Jennifer Wallace, *The Cambridge Introduction to Tragedy*, Cambridge University Press 2007, p.108.

23. Sarah Kane, *Complete Plays*, London, Bloomsbury Methuen Drama 2006, p.22.

24. Ibid., p.9.

25. Ibid., pp.47–8.

26. Ibid., p.51.

27. Wallace, *The Cambridge Introduction to Tragedy*, p.109.

28. Kane, *Complete Plays*, p.47.

29. Ibid., p.48.

30. Ibid.

31. Ibid., p.49.

32. Ibid., p.48.

33. See p.17 above.

34. See Davis, *Deracination*, chapter 5, especially pp.163–72, 183–91.

35. Kane, *Complete Plays*, p.142.

36. Ibid., p.205.

37. Ibid., p.212.

38. Ibid., p.213.

39. Ibid., p.218.

40. Ibid., p.220.

41. Ibid., p.245.

42. Ibid., p.243.

43. Raymond Williams, *Modern Tragedy*, London, Chatto and Windus 1966. The book was in part a riposte to Steiner's *Death of Tragedy*.

44. Ibid., p.75.

45. Ibid., p.59.

46. Ibid., pp.57–8.

47. Ibid., p.82.

48. Walter Stein, *Criticism as Dialogue*, Cambridge University Press 1969, p.237. Stein's book is an unjustly neglected set of reflections on the metaphysical and theological dimensions of the critical debates of the 1960s (especially in Cambridge) involving Williams, F. R. Leavis, L. C. Knights, and others.

49. Kane, *Complete Plays*, pp.57–8:

     IAN   What you doing?

     CATE   Praying. Just in case.

     IAN   Will you pray for me?

     CATE   No.

     IAN   When I'm dead, not now.

     CATE   No point when you're dead.

     IAN   You're praying for her.

     CATE   She's baby.

50. Ibid., pp.92–7.

51. Ibid., p.95; impossible to read without Kane's own suicide in mind.

52. Ibid., p.214.

53. Walter Benjamin, *The Origin of German Tragic Drama*, introduced by George Steiner, translated by John Osborne, London and New York, Verso 1998.

54. Ibid., p.113.

55. See Rowan Williams, *The Edge of Words: God and the Habits of Language*, London, Bloomsbury 2014, chapter 3.

5

Tragedy against Pessimism

Religious Discourse and Tragic Drama

I

The discussion of tragedy and the religious world-view—and, more specifically, tragedy and Christian theology—is one which exhibits, significantly, equal unease from both inside and outside religious systems. It is not only that secular critics warn against the distorting effect of theological interpretation in the reading of tragedy—I. A. Richards maintaining that 'The least touch of any theology that has a compensating Heaven to offer the hero is fatal',[1] George Steiner insisting that 'neither the Christian promise of salvation nor that of meliorist or utopian socialism...will generate tragedy',[2] Kathleen Sands arguing that 'tragedy is only apparent' from a Christian perspective, and 'losses can only be non-ultimate if the world and history are not of ultimate value to us'.[3] Theologians too have resisted the idea that what we have been calling the tragic imagination really belongs in a robustly religious framework. Thus, for example, the unfailingly intelligent and provocative John Milbank offers a strongly critical view of some attempts to 'naturalize' the tragic within theology in a treatment of the thought of Donald MacKinnon—generally agreed to be the major modern theological advocate of the tragic as an irreducible aspect of theological thinking.[4] MacKinnon argues in numerous places throughout his copious but unsystematic work that the tragic is intrinsic to Christian theology's workings—understanding the tragic as that element of the moral world which consistently confronts you with the fact that your decisions are made in a world you have *not* made, so that even the most purely intentioned acts regularly produce lethal damage. As one judicious recent study of him has suggested, he is translating into contemporary terms some of what a classical writer would have described as the workings of *tuche*, 'something that inserts itself between intention and consequence'[5]—what we casually call chance or luck. But for Milbank, the problem with MacKinnon's approach to the tragic is that it 'occasions a kind of *exit* from the narrative'[6] which blocks the path to anything we could call narrative resolution, a resolved *plot*. What Milbank is drawing attention to is MacKinnon's fascination with the pervasive ambiguities of choice and its effects: of any action in a narrative or drama we could say both that it might have been otherwise, and also that—even if it had been—the results would have been no less catastrophic. Linear narrative, moving towards resolution within one stream of development, slips out of focus because of an obsession with the ever-present shadow of unintended injury or catastrophe. For MacKinnon it is only in the destructively conflicting absolutes of tragic decision that we discover the nature of our human responsibility. Our salvation is simply in the fact that God, by becoming human in Jesus of Nazareth—and thus exposing himself to the exact and specific dilemmas of all human agents, the unavoidability of destructive shadows (and more) in all the actions we undertake—establishes that the divine is not destroyed by these limits and compromises but 'sustains' itself as a presence within our suffering.[7] Milbank goes on to make the intriguing suggestion that MacKinnon's version of the tragic is a kind of ontological transcription of 'the Church's minimal and very ambiguous social presence' in post-war Britain:[8] 'It could be that in such a society there is a tragic sundering of virtue into integrity of motive on the one hand and measurement of consequence on the other.'[9] That is to say, MacKinnon's problem is that he lacks a theory as to how non-destructive social practices may be created and maintained, and so is trapped in a standoff between purely individual motivation, with whatever integrity it can muster, and the inescapably corrupting and lethal realities of the public world: there is, in Hegel's terms, no *Sittlichkeit*, no recognition of the moral self in the other or in the communal discourse of humanity. At its most extreme, this seems to imply a near-Manichaean metaphysic, a fundamental sickness or rupture in reality; but at the same time, so Milbank allows, it illuminates the sick and ruptured character of late modernity, a cultural environment in which Manichaeism may be quite a tempting option.

We shall be returning to MacKinnon shortly; but at this point what is worth noting is Milbank's contention that to identify the tragic as an unavoidable, even inexorable, element in the moral universe is in effect to deny the significance of narrative itself—that is, of the idea that selves genuinely grow and change with the passage of time, and that there is an abiding hopefulness in this bare fact. Tragic narration, if it means what MacKinnon believes it does, is an attempt to empty out the very idea of a plot, a sequence of narrated events in which change occurs. In the 'tragic' world, *nothing really alters*: 'People change, and smile: but the agony abides', as Eliot wrote in 'The Dry Salvages'.[10] And if so, plot can never be more than a surface affair. What is fundamental is not capable of being plotted, even of being 'told'. MacKinnon and other 'tragic' theologians insist that the tragic imagination prevents theology from turning its attention away from the particularities of human history; but—so another forceful critic of MacKinnon, David Bentley Hart, has argued—tragedy 'turns attention not toward the one who suffers, but to the sublime background against which the drama is played out'.[11] It is the very opposite of a discipline of specific attention to pain and loss, universalizing (and so making abstract) the experience of suffering and thus also effectively legitimizing violence and conflict as the omnipresent conditions of human existence. It mystifies and so glamorizes violence.[12] It can deliver only 'a serene and chastened acceptance of where we are placed'.[13] A properly Christian theological discourse, in contrast, both insists on the unglamorous, sordid, and contingent nature of suffering and refuses to find meaning 'in' that reality, which is 'merely horrible, mad, everlastingly unjust';[14] it posits a real vindication, a real transfiguration that can be narrated—or rather, it does not *posit*, it witnesses to the event of resurrection. A theology of the cross alone, an affirmation that the death of Jesus is itself the moment of supreme meaningfulness, is a denial of the possibility of that real protest against suffering represented by the actual, historical reversal of death that is claimed for Jesus in the narratives of Easter. George Steiner and others are perfectly correct: Christianity is anti-tragic.

Hart's deconstruction of 'tragic' theology is powerful and in many aspects persuasive, providing a necessary corrective to some modern theological sentimentalities; but it rather takes for granted a view of classical tragedy that—ironically—sits light to its specifics (and he does not discuss Shakespeare or indeed any other post-classical dramatic texts). For Hart, Greek tragedy is essentially a set of variations on a single theme which has to do with the sovereignty of unfriendly fate and the unavoidability of appeasing a violent sacred order. 'Dionysus [in the *Bacchae* but also more generally] represents not a random instance of divine malice, but a force residing in the divine that is intrinsically violent; the power of the sacred, from which the city draws its sustenance and to which it must make oblations.'[15] And this sacred order is so fixed as to condemn human agents to irresoluble conflict and consequent suffering (as in *Antigone*). But this is at best a partial truth about some aspects of some classical tragedies: it has little to say about the careful interrogation of what lawfulness means, as we explored this in the first chapter, and little about the clear recognition in texts like the *Antigone* of the destructive effect of setting the sacred against itself; it is not a drama about 'the indeterminacy of moral meaning, or of moral responsibility'[16] in a world governed by indifferent deities and hostile fate. Hart seems to be working with just the model of Greek tragedy that Hegel so consistently objected to— tragic drama as a story of the conflict between noble humans and cruel external necessity. But he, like Milbank, does underline the risks of a tragic theology that is simply focused on the unrelieved pathos of human suffering and God's 'identification' with this. And that is less than what Christian theology has traditionally claimed for its business. Is there, then, a way of salvaging the insights or correcting the imbalance in Hart's (and—though to a less marked extent—Milbank's) essentialism about 'the tragic' without resigning from the theological enterprise altogether by absorbing the resurrection into the crucifixion, as MacKinnon and others are charged with doing?

To answer this needs a slightly closer look at what MacKinnon is actually arguing—not an easy task with a writer so dense in style and unsystematic in method. But take the fundamental question of 'plot' as it is articulated by Milbank: his problem with MacKinnon is that he finds the latter too ready to pull every narrative back to a seemingly inevitable corruption of intention in action, an incurring of some sort of guilt in the mere fact of decision-making. It has to be granted that MacKinnon's rhetoric is at times disturbingly close to the Manichaeism of which he stands accused, but his actual detailed argument is not so easily summed up in such terms; nor is this argument bound to the

private–public duality Milbank emphasizes (private integrity and public compromise). It should be clear from the examples MacKinnon
adduces that the horrors which may stem from good intentions are as
much personal and relational as they are public or social. At the root
of MacKinnon's concerns lie two basic truths: the fact of human
existence as necessarily limited (since this is a world we have not
made), and the fact of the irreversibility of time (subject of a brief but
immensely suggestive essay of 1975[17]). These are of course connected:
our ignorance of the future, which entails our ignorance of the effects
of our actions, is the way in which we perhaps most acutely experience the limits of our existence in a finite world; and in a finite world
where distorted desire has definitively taken root, this limitedness is
regularly (MacKinnon does not quite say 'necessarily') fleshed out in
the gulf which opens between intention and result, so much so that we
can say that this is somehow characteristic of being human. Irreversible
time is a basic assumption underlying how we talk about human
growth: we cease to think and feel in this particular way (the way that
characterizes childhood, say, or adolescence) and move into another
mode; but when we speak of *ceasing* to think and feel in certain ways,
we are recognizing that growth and loss or 'estrangement', to use
MacKinnon's word,[18] belong together. If, MacKinnon goes on, we
think of the life of Jesus as in some crucial sense 'innocent' (innocent
enough for him to be a credible intercessor for those who kill him), this
cannot mean that he did not grow in the way the rest of us do: he
must be familiar with estrangement, just as he must be familiar with
the human uncontrollability of the effects of his choices and acts.
And, as MacKinnon repeatedly points out,[19] part of the 'effect' of the
life and death and resurrection of Jesus is the damnation of Judas and
the history of anti-Semitism. In other words, Jesus's 'innocence' is not
a static freedom from damage and complicity in damage, a freedom
sustained by inaction: what matters is not that his acts are free from
the ambiguity and uncontrollable potential of all finite actions, not
even that he should be free from the bitterness of regret, but that he
continues to discover ways of embodying an unqualified compassion.[20]
In a grim theological 'thought experiment', MacKinnon examines[21]
some of the best-known parables of Jesus, the Good Samaritan and
the Prodigal Son, so as to draw out the possible moral ambiguities that
can be found in them: is the father in the Prodigal Son uncomfortably

like King Lear in his indifference to the unspectacular and inarticulate virtue of the elder son? Can the Samaritan be sure that his intervention is going to be effective rather than just a reflex bit of good behaviour? And if he is sure, what level of self-congratulation attends this? And what possibilities are there of creating damaging dependence by such an intervention, with its risk of being self-serving and self-reinforcing? One may raise an eyebrow or even smile at the macabre ingenuity with which MacKinnon develops these darkly novelistic alternative readings, but the point is quite simple: the world is complex enough not only to defeat but to corrupt good intentions. If we are looking for possibilities of actions that are free of such risk, we shall be either frustrated or dangerously self-deceived.

But what this shows is that it misses the mark to describe MacKinnon as rejecting plot and narrative. It is not that we are doomed to grave sin, or that virtue and honesty are inaccessible to us; we are not always already submerged in a timeless and inevitable guilt, so that the last word is a timelessly 'tragic' one. MacKinnon's argument is related to what was said in chapter 2 about the way tragic narrative reminds us that pain is not over and that 'The worst is not/ So long as we can say, "This is the worst."' To exist in time and its limits is to exist in a world where there is no *historical* end to risk and suffering, and thus to the likelihood of damage within any and every action. Yet this does not mean presupposing some supertemporal principle or existential curse. It is simply a matter of parsing what it means to recognize our finitude: narrative itself presupposes the irreversible passage of time and thus the omnipresence of loss. But that's the point: it is only in narrating it, 'plotting' it if you will, that it can be spoken of. What happens as a result of our decisions is not an abstract and identical calamity but always the specific kind of loss that *this* unique set of temporal conditions will generate.

So it could be said that MacKinnon is implying that the very act of narrating anything at all involves the possibility of *tragic* narration. The passage of time is a process of loss, *identified as such in the act of relating it.* Telling the story of the past is a representation of what both is and is not 'here'—certainly telling what is not here in the sense that even a first-person narration of the past creates a subject that is not the teller of the tale. Yet to recognize this element of loss or absence is not necessarily to be committed to a picture of finite existence as a struggle between fate and the noble but helpless subject. There are no subjects independent of awareness in time, and so to be a human subject is to be involved in understanding that growth, movement in time, entails a letting-go of past identities. That this is regularly accompanied by varying levels of grief does not mean that we are being deprived of some desirable good by a hostile environment; our grief is a recognition of the seriousness of the changes that have enabled us to tell the story as we actually do. The teller is not where the tale's action takes place, and this means, on the one hand, that the teller has lost the world that the agents of the tale inhabit, but on the other hand, that the teller is free from the confines of that world. Loss is, in a sense, what structures all narrative, to the extent that the teller is absent from the action of the tale. But MacKinnon goes rather further in connecting this loss with the fact that we have no control over what becomes of our actions: in narrating events, I tell the story of what I do and suffer, acknowledging that my past actions have been 'released' into a world of both consequences and meanings in which countless other processes, decisions, and determinations are at work. The same is obviously true of my present actions. But refusing to act because I cannot control interpretation and effect is a retreat from humanity itself, from its narrative and temporal character. In this sense it is true, as MacKinnon insists, that innocence is not available as a primordial gift to be preserved. None of this implies the fictions of noble frustration or edifying pain which Hart so rightly excoriates; the misery of unintended consequences, the absurd failure of good intentions, the routine bite of sorrow felt at lost time and severed relationships, all of these have more to do with what Hart sums up as the 'truly unbearable'—'the sheer contingency of evil, the injustice that destroys what is beautiful, the absolute, irrecuperable loss of the beloved'[22]—than with the 'sullen magnificence' which he (mistakenly) ascribes to Attic tragedy. Going back for a moment to Milbank's complaint about the occlusion in MacKinnon of the possibility of a 'resolved' plot, we can say that the issue is not whether 'resolution' is ever possible but whether we can craft or imagine a resolution that embraces the narrating of what cannot be mended—rather than a resolution which explains and so nullifies the tangles and injuries of what has been done or suffered. And it is clear enough that, unless you believe that resolution must mean an *unmaking* of the past (a far more serious attempt to exit from the world of narrative), it has to be thought about as a moment in which the strands of past narrative are so entwined as to mark a possible new stage in the story—not an absolute ending which obliterates the cost of what has gone before.

'There is a sense in which linear history is potentially tragic history, since what has been done cannot be undone':[23] Terry Eagleton in a recent book seems to be echoing MacKinnon as I have been reading him here. 'Resurrection', as he says, 'does not cancel the reality of crucifixion, or communism the horrors of the class society.'[24] But to say this is also to make the important point that the tragic imagination is not simply a form of pessimism:[25] if acts and events are uncontrollable in their effect, if we do not know what may flow from this or that happening, we are affirming in that acknowledgment that anguish and atrocity do not make a future impossible; they may shape a future that is profoundly, perhaps incurably damaged for at least some, but they do not stop things happening—and, more specifically, they do not stop things being spoken of. We are back with the question of how the representing of pain can be a new and transforming fact and also of how actual futures make the past of pain capable of narration in new ways that do not deny but 'relocate' what has happened. In other words, contrary to both Steiner and others from the non-Christian side and some of the more triumphalistic varieties of theology (and I do not include either Milbank or Hart under that designation), tragic imagination would be incompatible with Christian narrative only if tragedy were a form of pessimism and our proper reaction a form of Stoicism, reconciliation with the unbearable as inevitable. And MacKinnon's concern is surely less to avoid *any* kind of resurrection-based theology than to warn against any resolution that promises to cancel the tragic past.

II

All this talk of narrative reminds us that the tragedy and religion discussion is largely, if not quite exclusively, connected with Jewish and Christian theologies, for the simple reason that these traditions involve representations of the past as fundamental to their identity. These representations are both textual and liturgical; and in order to get some further purchase on the relation of these traditions to the tragic imagination, we shall be looking at three such representations—a directly dramatic narrative from Hebrew Scripture, a very slightly less directly dramatic one from Christian Scripture, and the most familiar ritual sequence in Christian practice: the Book of Job, the Gospel of John, and the Mass.

Job is unique in the books that compose the Hebrew Scriptures, in that it is essentially a series of speeches, enacting an intense controversy between Job and his friends, framed by brief narrative sections whose precise literary relationship with the speeches remains obscure. Part of the disturbing originality of the book is that it tells a story of appalling disaster that is inexplicable from the human point of view while framing it within another narrative—of negotiations in another world between God and the Prosecuting Angel ('Satan'); and, not content with this dangerously ironic stratagem, it presents Job, the victim of these disasters, as resolutely refusing the conventional theological explanation of his sufferings. It is as though a play like *Antigone* were to begin with a wager on Olympus about the likelihood of Antigone's fidelity to divine law in the face of mortal threat (and to end with her rescue and marriage to Haemon). That is to say, there is, provocatively, no mystery about Job's suffering as far as we, the readers or audience, are concerned; but there is total ignorance for the characters represented. This means that the entire long exchange of impassioned speeches is shot through with irony. Job's friends are determined to find an explanation for his calamities; but we, the audience, know that there is no explanation in the terms they are employing, no moral arithmetic at work, no tragic flaws being paid for. In the second chapter of this book, we were reflecting on how the audience at a drama knows what the characters cannot know; so here, too, with Job. But the further twist to the drama here is that Job is—so to speak—on the side of the audience without knowing it: he adamantly refuses to accept that his friends can possibly know what they claim to. He maintains his integrity by stubbornly maintaining his ignorance, as if, like us, he knows that there is no explanation to be had.

There is not much profit to be had in trying to work out whether Job is 'formally' a tragedy; but it is a work that displays what I have been calling tragic imagination in several ways. Its opening narrative, having set up a situation of apparently maximal stability and prosperity, exposes its fragility simply by exposing to us the debate in the court of heaven in which God decides to prove to Satan that disinterested piety and virtue are possible: that suffering need not destroy faith. But Job, having begun with something like resignation (1.21: 'The Lord gave and the Lord has taken away; may the name of the Lord be praised'), moves on to protest his innocence with ever greater fierceness, and to demand not explanation but *vindication*; he demands that his record be scrutinized in open court, so that if God has a case against him it can be tested. 'I sign now my defence—let the Almighty answer me; let my accuser put his indictment in writing' (31.35). His response is anything but Stoic. He insists on clearing his name and will not accept that he must deny what he knows to be true of himself— that he has not deserved this suffering as a punishment. This is what he knows, and this is what his friends claim to know more about than he does—and more than we as audience do, since we know from the start that this is not a story of sin or failure bringing disaster in its wake. It is about the sheer gulf between divine and human perspective. And the final response of God, speaking 'out of the storm' (38.1), is, famously, a kind of counter-refusal: God refuses as stubbornly and eloquently as does Job to make a moral case for Job's suffering, and (it seems) simply browbeats him by displaying the incomprehensible complexity of the created order.

This, though, is not all: he rebukes Job's friends, comparing what they have said unfavourably with Job's words. Job has 'spoken the truth about me' (42.7). Job has called for a court hearing, confident that God will vindicate him as innocent, and God's overwhelming intervention (as readers of the book sometimes fail to see) is precisely such a vindication: there is indeed no ground in Job's behaviour for the suffering that has fallen upon him. In other words, innocence and guilt are irrelevant to suffering, as Hegel claims they are in classical tragedy.[26] Job, no less than Hegel's classical tragic agents, enacts and narrates who and what he is, and in response God enacts and narrates who *he* is. God is the energy of diverse, superabundant creation, Job is a finite agent; whatever their relationship, it cannot be one of tidy moral reward or the promise of security within a finite and unimaginably complex world. If God is to be loved or served, it *must* be 'for nothing'—which is what God has sought to establish in his 'wager' with the Prosecutor (1.9ff). But, as if the author of Job had foreseen Milbank's critique of MacKinnon, there is a final 'resolution', and Job is granted a renewed prosperity. The plot ties itself up neatly; but by this time we know both that Job's new property and family are not final rewards for virtue, since they can have no more intrinsic stability than anything else in the fragile order of finite being. The resolution of the plot is not an answer to any question, and the vindication of Job is not the visible re-establishing of his prosperity. In dramatic terms, it is a little like the 'resolution' that occurs at the end of *The Winter's Tale*: the child Mamilius is still dead, Hermione embraces her husband but has nothing to say to him;[27] the offer of renewed relationship, restored joy, is something that silences and bewilders, and certainly does not abolish or soften the history of terrible loss. To put it slightly differently, the resolution is not something that the plot necessarily generates: Shakespeare's notorious readiness in the late plays to cast plotted plausibility to the winds is a way of saying what the end of Job appears to be pointing to: suffering may be displaced by prosperity, by happiness, but also it may not. 'Happy endings', as in *The Winter's Tale*, do not change the story as it has unfolded, and so do not absolve what has happened; they simply continue a narrative in which pain and atrocity are not automatically the last word—any more than well-being is. So what is to be said or understood or 'told' about suffering cannot be rendered in terms of book-keeping—so much compensation for so much pain; and the implication is that any particular episode of suffering cannot be the subject of a simple rational calculus, as if it were the payment of a debt (incurred by some kind of sin or disobedience to God or the gods) or as the incurring of a debt (obliging God or the gods to recompense the sufferer). As we saw with *Lear* in chapter 2, the moral world resists this language of debt; and tragic narrative is in part a way of reinforcing such resistance.

Tragic representation in this perspective is what represents extreme pain and moral disaster neither as inevitable nor as curable. It does not assume that there are never anything but evil outcomes in mortal life, or that we are doomed to inflict pain; but it does not assume either that, when evil outcomes occur, there is some moral explanation or compensatory framework in which the evil can be relativized and the damage undone. To recall Martha Nussbaum's phrase, there may be 'healing without cure'—that is, there may be a future in which the unaltered memory of hurt comes to be lived with in unpredictable ways, without wholly destructive consequences. But to arrive at such a moment (so Job seems to suggest) you have first to give up any hope of explanation or compensation. What makes this kind of narration 'tragic' is not that it insists on some fundamental metaphysical priority or necessity to failure and suffering (the 'absolute tragedy' model discussed in the preceding chapter), but its focus on the cost of what we do not know, cannot know, or refuse to know. We do not and cannot know how our choices affect our world, and we cannot keep ourselves or others safe from the contingencies of the world or the results of our actions; we are equally liable (like Job's friends) to refuse to know our ignorance, and so to compound the world's misery by looking for moral accounts of events which hold sufferers straightforwardly responsible for their condition. As has often emerged in this discussion, mourning, the articulation of plain loss, is something that has to be given its own room, its own integrity. Explanation and compensation suggest that there is something somewhere that makes mourning inappropriate: tragedy in contrast seeks a voice for appropriate mourning, affirming neither absolute guilt nor absolute innocence among the agents of the drama, but only their location in the historical world in which debt and calculus do not determine outcomes.

In the Christian narrative, of course, the central episode of Jesus's humiliation and death by torture stands as a perpetual caution against the world of moral calculus (and at least one of his recorded sayings, in Luke 13.1–5, rejects an exact proportion of guilt to suffering in favour of a general warning against the risk of living ignorantly in self-focused or self-satisfied ways). There is a monumental tragic irony in the very grammar of this narrative, which tells of the most dramatic possible schism between self and truth, and the maximal degree of misrecognition. But of all the biblical narratives setting out this story, it is the Gospel of John that is generally agreed to be the most self-conscious in bringing these ironies to the fore. It begins by setting the scene against a timeless backdrop: the story we are to hear is the story whose subject is eternal and creative agency, and we are immediately told that this agency is unrecognizable to creation in general and to those in particular who have been most directly touched by it. 'He came to that which was his own, but his own did not receive him' (John 1.11)—a perfect instance, incidentally, of MacKinnon's point that the unavoidable ironies of Jesus's story as related by John can be twisted into entirely unironic grounds for murderous anti-Judaism by those who fail to hear the nature of the irony entailed (that those who believe they know where God's favour is to be found are those most deeply in the dark).

As the story unfolds, repeated reference is made to the tension between what those around Jesus believe they know and what Jesus, and we as hearers of his story, know. 'He knew what was in each person' (John 2.25) and so has no illusions about the trustworthiness of human perception and commitment. The possibility of truthful vision has arrived in the world, but human agents prefer not to know (3.19–20). Those around him study the sacred texts as a means to find eternal life, but do not recognize the subject of those texts when he is in front of them (5.39). When he has gone away, there will be those who recognize too late what they have ignored; but those who look for him will not be able to find him because they cannot come to where he is (7.34). Jesus's coming is intended to help the blind see and to make those who say they can see blind: their claim that they can see seals their guilt, once the light has actually been given (9.41). And there are the ironies in the dialogue itself—the High Priest declaring that one man must die for the people (11.50), Pilate's derisive, 'You are a king, then!', and, most famously of all, 'What is truth?' (18.37, 38). Examples could be multiplied, but the point is clear enough. John's narrative is systematically underlining the tension between what is conventionally claimed as known or knowable and the presence of truth itself. The language that is in theory prepared or equipped to tell the truth about the truth, so to speak, is shown to be incapable of holding what it purports to convey; more than that, it acts so as actively to try and silence the truth. Human action and speaking deny their context and foundation, and the source of life (1.4) is inexorably pushed towards death. It is often remarked that John's Jesus shows few signs of distress in the face of death, in contrast to the depictions of intense struggle and anguish in the other gospels; but the narrative focus is precisely not on how Jesus 'feels' about his death, but on the bare fact that human agency all around Jesus is in revolt against the embodiment of life. It is not the *intensity* of suffering that matters here, but the identity of the sufferer.

This means that the Gospel of John is 'tragic' not simply in the sense that it tells a story of catastrophe (though it does) but that it dramatizes the interwoven contingency and necessity of pain or failure in the sharpest way imaginable. The world is such that personalized and substantive divine goodness cannot be secure against ignorance and misrecognition; worse still, it is the very fact that personalized divine goodness is present that triggers misrecognition. So different is actual divinity from its representations that it can only appear as the enemy of God (as Jesus says to his disciples in 16.2, 'Anyone who kills you will think they are offering a service to God'). Yet at the same time, only in the working out of this misrecognition can recognition occur: the narrating of the ultimate catastrophe in which truth is displayed as the victim of the world we know is the precondition of seeing that the world we know is indeed lethally contingent. It is in the light of this revelation that we learn to mourn without reservation, but also to be attentive to what is now making it possible to tell the story of catastrophe. In John's Gospel, Jesus predicts the coming of the 'Spirit of Truth' (14.26, 16.13–15) who will recall the history of Jesus and present it afresh to the disciples: by means of this retelling, the catastrophe is both shown for what it is—the most complete of metaphysical ruptures—and shown to be 'speakable', capable of being thought, followed, woven in to a continuing narration that will alter the possibilities. In common with the tragic texts we have been considering earlier in this book, the Gospel of John dramatizes the connection between ignorance and refusal of the truth, loss of identity and capacity to speak, awareness of unmanageable contingency and the emergent possibility of new speech (not to reverse this history or explain it but to mourn appropriately and in so doing find a place to stand that is not wholly paralysed by the memory of atrocity). Whatever may be said about this, it is rather different from the impatient versions of religious metaphysics deployed by secular critics to distance Christian language from the tragic. Equally, it does not amount to the kind of metaphysical inscription of 'necessary' guilt, failure, or pain to which Milbank and Hart object.

John's Gospel is one of the key texts for the theology of the Swiss Catholic thinker, Hans Urs von Balthasar, who has written a good deal on the subject of drama in general and tragedy in particular as a theological theme.[28] He comes very close to the 'Manichaean' picture of a terminally divided cosmos in his consistent emphasis on the story of Christ's death as presenting a sort of eternal tension between Father and Son in the life of God as trinity. Jesus is for him the ultimate tragic hero: he is the sufferer who is 'affirmed by the divine'[29] despite the fact that his human suffering is brought about by a collision between divine will and human survival, in certain specified circumstances (a formulation that works well for the book of Job as for the gospel story); but this collision is also, and crucially, the collision between Jesus, the incarnate Son, as a human agent, and the heavenly Father of Jesus. The Father is necessarily absent and impotent in the face of the Son's historical suffering, since that suffering is precisely the Father's will; it is what brings about the Father's purpose of healing and renewal for all the human world. On the one hand, the Father cannot intervene to save the Son without betraying his purpose, and so betraying himself; on the other, the Son embodied in the human Jesus must be unequivocally faithful to a mission which is his very identity. In classical Christian theology, Jesus's humanity has its particular, unique historical identity simply because it has been taken as the vehicle in history in which the eternal outpouring of God's life is embodied. What makes Jesus who he is is the bestowal of divine life in the world. But the world is a world that has chosen to shut out divine life, and it is what *it* is as a 'godless' space, violently closing itself off from the divine and thus violently rejecting divine life when it is embodied in the world. There is therefore a multiple necessity to the story of Jesus's suffering: the cross stands where it does because of God's eternal purpose and character, because of Jesus's identity as 'sent' on behalf of God's purpose, embodying divine gift, and because of the world's self-inflicted closure against God. If there were a hint that Jesus could, so to speak, open a gap in the world's fabric to keep himself safe, he would be violating these three points of unavoidable constraint. When, on the cross, he cries, 'Why have you forsaken me?', he is in effect declaring that he himself has not abandoned his mission, not violated the logic of 'being God' in a world like this; that is why he is there, dying in agony. He is devoted to speaking and acting for God in the face of the Godless world, and so cannot turn his face away from that world back to a divine presence located somewhere else ('Heaven'). If he has not abandoned his mission to embrace that world and to restore human capacity for God from within the human world, he has not abandoned God his Father; and—to complete this heady and intensely woven theological pattern—if he has not abandoned his Father and his will is one with the Father's will, this cry of agony is a kind of witness to the unbroken unity of God as Father and God as Jesus Christ: only in the particularities of this human catastrophe, the rejection and killing of Jesus, can we see how such a union is real.

There could, for Balthasar (and for any theologian), be no more extreme a statement of the tragic than this. The self-consistency of the divine life—including God's will for the good of creation—requires that life to be lived within a creation radically divided from God by sin; and so the life lived by God in creation is lived in a condition of extreme distance from God, at the heart of the condition of contingent vulnerability. In Balthasar's framework, to say that Christ is the supreme tragic hero is to say not that he is a human being who happens to suffer more than anyone else in history (though Balthasar can sometimes write as if this *is* what he is claiming), but that there could be no more radical a rupture in the fabric of reality than God alienated from God. And for Balthasar it is the Christian doctrine of the trinity that—by positing eternal differentiation within the divine life—allows for this 'tragic' rupture to occur without entailing a kind of tragic division within God that would have somehow to be overcome,[30] a collapse of divine integrity into contradiction and opposition. For Balthasar, John's Gospel is the narrative articulation of all this: Jesus does entirely what the Father wills for the sake of human well-being and absolution, and this loyalty to the divine will entails an apparent abnegation of divine power and liberty in the face of human violence (see, for example, John 5.19, 8.28–9,15.18–25, 16.2, 18.36 for various iterations of the theme that Jesus does what the Father does and so is never strictly speaking abandoned; that this involves inviting the murderous hatred of those who are unwilling to confront truth; and that there is no human defence against such hatred). His infinite freedom is the freedom to accept the required sacrifice of his life without rebellion (10.17–18), so that his death becomes the supreme sign of his liberty.

These are complex speculations, and they have not gone without challenge from some; but they bring into sharp focus aspects of tragic representation that have been in view throughout our discussion. The Christian narrative may indeed help in identifying some of what is distinctive in tragedy because of its refusal of two profoundly 'anti-tragic' stances. Christian theology—contrary to some caricatures of it—does not require us to suppose that suffering is cancelled or even compensated by the hope of ultimate reconciliation (any more than Hegel's scheme—contrary to some caricatures of it—involves a conclusion that everything is 'really' all right). The Christian future is not simply a deferred rescue operation.[31] Equally, because Christian discourse does not accept the possibility of 'absolute tragedy' (as defined in the previous chapter), it affirms the possibility of mourning—the articulation of loss, the 'telling' of pain, in a way that allows catastrophe and atrocity to become culturally thinkable: not explicable or justifiable but material for self-awareness and mutual recognition. The paradox of claims about absolute tragedy is that they make *tragedy as cultural product* unintelligible, because of a fear that this cultural negotiation of the memories of terror is a kind of denial of their seriousness. As we shall see further in the final chapter of this book, the deeper risk is of rendering suffering literally unspeakable—and so of silencing the voice of the specific historical sufferer in the name of an absolute and timeless necessity. In contrast, the theological perspective affirms that fundamental reality and agency, divine truth itself, is torn apart in and by human history and yet brings itself together and is not destroyed.

But there is another dimension to the convergence and focus here. Job and John are both works which, without being formally dramas, operate with extensive dramatic exchange, advancing through dialogues and staged debates that are regularly freighted with irony. They remind us that tragedy is a kind of performance, a process in words that plays with the distance between speakers in the narrative and spectators or audience. We have already seen that, to attend or 'assist at' a tragedy, we covenant certain fixed responses, certain habits of silence and restraint; we accept that we are being acted upon, while retaining the perspective that allows us to be aware of irony and multiple meaning. We are bound to the time taken by the drama, yet in an important sense we are not simply 'contemporary' with the action of the drama. We saw at the start of this book that the liturgical setting of Greek tragedy is an essential aspect of its workings; and it is time to examine the parallels and differences between Christian liturgical action and the tragic 'liturgies' evoked earlier in this book. From the beginning, Christian practice has been characterized by ritual actions of a very specific shape, representing the transition from one world to another. In baptism, the candidate undergoes a ritual death by 'drowning', immersion under water; in the Eucharist, the community is identified variously with the first generations to whom the gospel was proclaimed (as hearers of Hebrew Scripture and of Paul's letters), with those in general directly contemporary with Jesus, more specifically with the disciples in the Upper Room at the Last Supper (destined collectively and individually to betray Jesus), with those whom he feeds after his resurrection, and with his own eternal prayer to the Father. We are made aware of the continuity of divine promise, and aware also, at every stage, of that which, on the human side, breaks the effect of divine promise. We continue to expose ourselves to hearing because we shall never have heard enough; having heard, we typically revert to un-hearing and un-seeing, and so must repeat endlessly the story of divine constancy and human infidelity. When the breaking of bread is performed as at the Last Supper, we as 'audience'/congregation know that what it *really* makes present is the terminal breaking of body and relationship that occurs in the crucifixion; we know what the disciples at the Last Supper don't know. Equally, when the bread is broken in memory of betrayal and death, we know what the witnesses to the death of Jesus don't know, that his agony becomes nourishment through his own repetition and re-presentation of the story after the resurrection. This is most vividly portrayed in the Emmaus story in Luke 24, where the—unrecognized—Jesus who has returned from death both re-tells the tale of previous history as a foreshadowing of his death, and then breaks bread afresh with disciples who are in flight from the place of his death. Once again, a deeply ironic narrative form is deployed: we know what the journeying disciples don't; yet at the same time this irony is turned back onto us as 'audience'. What is it then that *we* don't know or see 'in the breaking of bread' here and now?

In these and other ways, the structure of the Eucharist echoes what has been said about the tragic liturgy of the ancient city. It represents a story of extreme rupture and dissolution in the common life: Jesus dies abandoned by most of those closest to him, the community, the 'city' he has created is dissolved by this betrayal, and he dies in agony of body and spirit. More than that, though

less explicitly, what is represented is an apparent rupture in the
divine action—the abandonment *by God* of God's human embodiment ('My God, my God, why have you forsaken me?'), and so the
apparent schism in divine self-consistency or fidelity. In the context
of social meaning taken for granted by Jesus and his religious culture, divine faithfulness, covenanted loyalty, is crucial to the understanding both of divine nature and of the identity of the chosen
human community: to question it is to question the foundation of
the legitimacy of the chosen people. Like classical tragedy, this is a
narrative which presses to the extreme the possibility of a radical
fragmentation of 'lawful' common life. In this perspective, the
eucharistic representation does exactly what Simon Goldhill identifies as a central aspect of classical tragedy: its task is to 'make
difficult the assumptions of the values of the civic discourse'. And
it does so, once again like classical tragedy, by returning to a familiar story in order to discover what is still unknown about it—or
rather what is still unknown about us as hearers of the story. The
ironies presented in the dramatic narration invite us as audience to
scrutinize ourselves, to learn how to see ourselves with greater
ironic clarity, acknowledging what we do not know of ourselves.
Mourning, in the form of repentance, is tightly interwoven with
the process by which solidarity is reconstituted through the dramatic action: our solidarity in betrayal with the disciples at the
Last Supper becomes a solidarity with those reconnected with
each other in the post-resurrection encounters like the Emmaus
story. Once the civic discourse has been dismantled in the experience
of catastrophe, it is then re-founded by the divine announcement of a
new state of recognition and justice, by the declaration that the violent
rivalry which controls itself by finding scapegoats has been definitively
refused and supplanted. As 'Athens' emerges from tragic narrative in
the Greek theatre, so 'the Church' emerges from the narrative enacted
in the Christian sacrament. And the fact that *something emerges* is no
more an argument for the non-tragic character of Christian representation than the divine institution of Athenian law is an argument
against the tragic character of the *Oresteia*.

   In the simplest terms: the fact that the Christian narrative does not
have a conclusion that is unrelieved grief or disaster does not make it
non-tragic or anti-tragic. Kathleen Sands's comment, quoted earlier,

about how any treatment of loss as 'non-ultimate' is bound to imply that our own valuation of world and history must be of less than ultimate significance or seriousness begs the question of what it would mean to say that loss was indeed '*ultimate*'. It should be possible to say that loss is in an important sense irremediable, beyond compensation, without concluding that it is *the* unsurpassable category of human speech and experience. Loss is appalling because world and history matter; no reason to dispute that. But if world and history matter in such a way, are we bound to absolutize moments of loss and say that they necessarily silence the possibility of representation that sets out to be not consoling but at least 'enabling'? A too ready acceptance of the language of ultimacy here would seem to involve accepting a set of very contestable ideas about tragedy that will not stand up well to the actualities of tragic drama in its history—the idea, for example, that tragedy must be a representation of suffering or atrocity that is devoid of hope, value, or future. In Terry Eagleton's provocative phrase, it might be that 'the exemplary case of hope is tragedy':[32] catastrophic suffering, moral and political disaster and so on present us with the stark question of what actually *matters*, whatever happens; but to discover what matters in this way is itself a ground of hope, a recognition of what disaster cannot entirely destroy. 'Tragedy cuts deeper than pessimism', according to Eagleton, because it tells us why this or that particular loss is so appalling. If loss is necessary, that is as destructively anti-tragic a conclusion as to say that loss is capable of compensation through a happy ending.

III

This is why some of those works that are sometimes interpreted as formally Christian tragedies are more problematic than such a designation might allow. Milton's *Samson Agonistes* sets out to tell a biblical story in the form of a Greek tragedy: the blind hero led on stage to sit and ruminate and receive various interlocutors at once recalls *Oedipus at Colonus*, and the Chorus's theological interjections are clearly meant to echo the set-piece invocations and hymnic meditations that we hear from Sophocles' Chorus. Milton's own introduction to the drama (or dramatic poem; it is unlikely that he ever intended it to be performed) deliberately challenges comparison with the great Attic tragedians, and there is no doubt that his flexible, intense, and vivid rhetoric has something of the quality of the Greek masters. Samson makes an eloquent appeal against his fate—especially his blindness, cutting him off from light, which is 'the prime work of God'[33]—and insists that he has been loyal to God's will, except in betraying the secret of his strength to Dalila; when she appears to ask his forgiveness, she is uncompromisingly rebuffed and blamed by Samson and the Chorus for her seduction of him. Her own account of the pressure she has felt from her family and people—her own attempt, we could say, to present herself in a 'tragic' mode—is dismissed. Samson's degree of culpability is a grey area in the poem, with the Chorus more than once reverting to the incomprehensibility of divine decrees: God is not bound by his law or reason ('with his own Laws he can best dispence' (314), 'Down Reason then, at least vain reasonings down' (321)), and the pattern of his favour or disfavour is not to be mapped by human minds. All we can know is his power ultimately to vindicate his justice—as he does spectacularly in the final act of Samson's life, when he pulls down the idolatrous temple on the heads of the assembled Philistines. In the light of this, the Chorus can declare that 'Nothing is here for tears' (1721), and end in the confidence that 'All is best' (1745).

It is a passionately sustained work; but it stands at some distance from the understanding of tragedy we have been exploring so far. Most notably, perhaps, there is the discordance between the concluding 'Nothing is here for tears' and the 'weep no more' of the ending of *Oedipus at Colonus*[34]—not to mention the eschatological wiping away of tears in the last book of the Bible.[35] Milton's Chorus denies that grief is appropriate, where Sophocles simply urges silence after mourning and the acceptance that all things are in the hands of the divine. In other words, it is as if Milton refuses mourning itself; the tragic narrative, for him, is ultimately a mistaken way of appropriating catastrophe; lament and protest (as in Samson's opening speeches and his replies to his father) give way to resistance and ultimately revenge in the name of God. At the end, the slate is cleared: if God has appeared inconsistent, he has now salvaged his reputation; if Samson has been guilty, he has now purged his sin. We as audience are exhorted to patience rather than self-scrutiny; this is a forcefully and unapologetically non-ironic telling of the story of suffering. As such, it invites some of the unease expressed by secular critics about religious appropriations of tragedy: it could be rendered as a narrative of temporary failure and pain fully and unambiguously resolved by a reversal of fortune, even though that reversal entails a kind of sacrificial death. This, of course, is not all there is to this intensely animated text: Dalila's appeals to Samson read almost as an appeal to allow genuine tragic irresolution into a story of simple rights and wrongs. But if Milton's literary imagination could not deny a hearing for this appeal, Milton's ultimate ideological verdict is that it must be an error to look for ambiguity here. Suffering and death are ascribable to God's inscrutable purpose—with Milton standing firmly on the side of those who see God's will in positivist terms, an unconstrained prescription of certain acts (rather than, as in other sorts of seventeenth-century theology, an expression of unchanging divine nature); and so suffering and death are not contingent, but deliberate divine 'strategies'.

Another dramatic work of almost exactly the same vintage as *Samson* has sometimes been presented as a case of specifically Christian tragedy. In a recent essay,[36] Simon Critchley has offered a notably insightful and challenging reading of Racine's *Phèdre* in these terms, defining 'Christian tragedy' as 'an essentially anti-political tragedy that would consist in the rejection of the worldly order and the radical separation of subjectivity and the world'.[37] Phaedra, married to Theseus and unrequitedly in love with her stepson Hippolytus, is presented to us by Racine from the very beginning as consumed with self-disgust, paralysed by 'languor', the drastically enervating effect of an erotic obsession wholly prevented from being consummated, and feeding on the vital forces of Phaedra's bodily existence. She is literally dying of love, in the sense that her passion cannot turn outwards; and because it is illicit and excessive in every conceivable way, it is appropriate that it threatens her very life. For Phaedra, the bare fact of bodily existence is torment; the divine Sun, source of all life, looks on her and the 'doomed race' of which she is part with appalled dismay (I.iii).[38] The gods have made her but predestined her to be 'depraved' (II.v). What is more, she can have no hope of escape from this torment through death, since an uncompromising judgement awaits (IV.6). As Critchley notes, quoting Lucien Goldmann's classic study of the theological world which Racine occupied, '[T]he God of tragedy is a God who is always present and always absent':[39] Phaedra has nowhere to hide from the universal light of the Sun, to whom her wicked desire is plain and open; but there is no *agency* that can act to separate her from the guilt bound up in her identity as a conscious subject. Critchley connects this with the rhetoric of Augustine's *Confessions*, arguing that the saint's awareness of an inescapable but unacceptable desire that is transparent to the eyes of God is exactly what Phaedra experiences— but without Augustine's possibility of a rescue at the hands of divine grace. Phaedra lives out an 'exitless existence',[40] which is sensed as 'not anxiety or fear, but rather *horror*'.[41] And this is connected by Critchley with Heidegger's analysis of fundamental inauthenticity in human existence ('Existence is that load or burden to which I am enchained and in which I languish'):[42] all human agents are 'indebted' to a history beyond their control or understanding, and this constitutes a central lack at the heart of humanity.

This is a complex reading. In essence, what is being argued is that the human agent is always already deprived of control. I am thrown, projected (as Heidegger liked to say), into a condition in which I can make no meaning for myself. My sense of myself is disconnected from the givenness of what I can discern around me in the world of nature. What I desire is thus at odds with this surrounding complex of given processes. And whether I theoretically accept it or reject it, I am wrongfooted, shut out from any given order or intelligibility and thus from living in a truth that is more than my private desire. I may seek to escape the world or I may embrace it, but it will always be the case that I am outside it. Nothing is 'given' for my subjectivity, and to be truthful to this subjectivity is to acknowledge this alienation, which I have not chosen or created but cannot avoid. If, like Racine and his characters, I believe myself to be living in the presence not only of a given world but of a transcendent and all-seeing God, I have no space for escape or absolution.

Phaedra is articulating not guilt over a specific transgression but the paralysed recognition of an always-already guilty subjectivity. But this also means that if you ask *whose* tragedy *Phèdre* is, the answer is not 'Phaedra' or 'Hippolytus' or any other particular character. The tragedy is the world's: truthful subjectivity, like Phaedra's, cannot live in the world (we should probably have to say, in *any* world), so that Phaedra's death is the death of 'the polis, the city, the state, the political order'.[43]

Critchley notes that the near-contemporaneous *Samson* likewise leaves the public order in ruins, a meaningless charade that is fit only for repudiation and destruction—always Philistia, never a redeemed Israel (one of the themes of *Samson* is indeed the fact that Israel has not been saved or changed by Samson's actions, nor is there any hope that the catastrophic and bloody ending will alter this). Our common tragedy, which Phaedra forces on our attention, is that we are never at one with ourselves, never an object to ourselves like other objects, located ('thrown' in Heideggerian terms) in the world, yet not part of it. This is what it is to be reflective; and in this sense, Critchley echoes Hegel in suggesting that tragedy is intrinsic to thought itself; and the residual question is what we do with all this if it is no longer possible to believe in God. Racine's God is necessarily both omnipresent and entirely silent—and it is a short step to concluding that language about God can have no content. But if so, all we are left with is a subjectivity that cannot exist with integrity in the exchange and calculation of the public world, the world of speech and negotiation (as we have already noted, Sarah Kane's reworking of the story effectively presents Hippolytus as the mouthpiece of a very similar aporia: existence is beyond forgiveness). There is not even the faint hope that—whatever may have been the tragedy of pre-Christian souls like Phaedra—grace may somehow rescue us by affirming a connection between the isolated self and the divine, creating a 'world' of relatedness within, alongside, and beyond the world we know.

This intriguing discussion highlights a number of significant features in Racine's drama—not least its distance from the classical tragic form as well as the original classical story. The concluding action by which the bereaved Theseus adopts his dead son's intended bride as his daughter is a pale reflection of Greek tragedy's laborious reconnection of shattered bonds and expectations. And earlier on, it is very noticeable that Phaedra, in I.v and III.i, initially accepts Oenon's argument that she must rally herself to secure her son's succession to the throne and then declares that she cannot think about the governing of a state when she cannot govern herself, and yearns to hand over public power to Hippolytus. She does indeed understand her suffering as cutting her off from the possibility of action and decision; and her rhetoric about her own guilty passion is regularly about a divine force which predestines her to this agony. Almost nothing in the play is about actual human decision: fate and curse have taken over. How far this reflects the deep determinism of Racine's Jansenist piety is a matter still debated by critics. Roland Barthes proposed that the underlying theme of *Phèdre* was the human duty to absolve God: Phaedra, by giving imaginative form to her predetermined, shapeless, and causeless existential guilt, provides God with an excuse for her damnation.[44] But it is not clear that this can be so simply linked with a distinctively 'Christian' agenda for tragic narrative as Critchley suggests. It is certainly true that part of the Christian perspective in tragedy we have sketched in this chapter has to do with our inheritance of a complex of causal chains we do not control, so that the outcome of our acts is likewise beyond our control. MacKinnon's relentless stress on the limits of moral strategy and the unknowable outcome of even the most purportedly selfless and salvific actions is no less stringent a reading of our human situation than Heidegger's. But there are two aspects of our earlier discussion which might put a question mark against Critchley's reading of Racine as paradigmatically a Christian tragedian. The first is the bare fact that suffering can be narrated and thus communicated or imaginatively shared; that it can become (as it was expressed earlier) a *cultural* fact. A reading purely in terms of existential guilt, identity as burden and trap, would have to be modified as soon as this becomes a matter of language and representation: identity is reconfigured in exchange and recognition. Telling the story of catastrophe creates a world, and in a certain sense enables action in a world, action that is a critique of fatalism and an affirmation of value. The second is our old friend, irony: if tragedy is the sheer burden of existence, that would leave us with another non-ironic model. All we (as audience) can come to know in the dramatic encounter is what the tragic protagonist knows: the unbearable nature of finitude. There is no generative gap between what the dramatic agent knows and what we know; there is one lesson to be learned, and it is about the disastrous nature of finite existence as such. But tragedy in a fuller and more historically nuanced sense refuses this despair of finitude by the mere fact of narration, *following on* from the record of horror and failure; and to do this requires irony, the awareness of ignorance in both the dramatic characters and the observing audience. Racine's—or Critchley's—Phaedra is aware of her unfreedom, and we as audience can't disagree. But—if our analysis throughout this book has been correct—part of the force of tragic drama is that audiences are invited to disagree with the characters.

I leave on one side the quite complicated question of whether Critchley is right in his reading of Augustine (I have some substantial reservations about this); but I think he is largely right in his reading of Racine. *Phèdre*, like *Samson*, is an extraordinarily concentrated dramatic poem; as Critchley says,[45] Phaedra is 'the only substantial character onstage', as is Samson for most of Milton's poem (making some allowance for Dalila). But one consequence of this is that a strictly *dramatic* process is harder to discern: what is actually brought to light and developed in the exchanges of speech within the drama? Secrets are disclosed, reactions are depicted; but nothing alters in the fundamental fact of Phaedra's self-disgust and commitment to self-cancellation, and nothing therefore *happens* in the drama. Critchley is right to say that Racine pushes the boundaries of the genre.[46] But this also means that the various ways in which the Christian narrative illuminates and intersects with the tragic imagination are not much in evidence. If the reading suggested of John's Gospel is correct, the schism in reality for a Christian imagination is not between subject and world but between God as the eternal will for healing and God as the compromised and vulnerable agent within history who can change history only by renouncing power or security or success. What the narrative of Christ's suffering does is to invite our ironic appreciation of the scale of misrecognition that is involved in human authority judging the divine: an appreciation that entails a particularly intense self-questioning. This scheme proposes a *prima facie* rupture between self and truth, between world and subject, that is every bit as serious as what Critchley sees in Racine; but it puts into question the way in which tragic subject and indifferent world are imagined, as rival frames of moral reference, by insisting on two things. The first is the need to recognize our misrecognition of the self itself. We must go beyond the injured and doomed subjectivity of Racine's early modern self and reopen questions about speech and communal identity—and thus about the possibility of another kind of world. The second is the need to understand the implications of 'telling' suffering, creating dramatic representations of human disaster; this implies (if we think back to earlier comments on *King Lear*) that there is a world of understanding in which pain can be spoken and shown, though not by that means softened or denied or consoled. And the distinctive representation that is the Christian Eucharist displays both these points with clarity.

In short, it is very far from established that Judaeo-Christian representation and tragic imagination must be regarded as incompatible. If it is acknowledged—as it is by critics as different as Steiner and Critchley—that there is something about tragic narrative that demands acknowledgment of the 'sacred' dimension, we should not be surprised to find that the specifics of this Judaeo-Christian thinking and 'telling' throw into clear relief some fundamental features of tragic drama. But this will be clear only if we resist the essentialism about tragedy (on the part of theologians as much as literary interpreters) that draws our attention away from the specifics not only of actual human pain but of actual human representation of pain.

Notes

1. I. A. Richards, *The Principles of Literary Criticism*, London, Kegan Paul, Trench, Trubner 1924, p.246.
2. George Steiner, 'Absolute Tragedy', *No Passion Spent: Essays 1978–1996*, London, Faber 1996, p.139.
3. Kathleen Sands, 'Tragedy, Theology, and Feminism in the Time After Time', in Rita Felski (ed.), *Rethinking Tragedy*, Baltimore MD, Johns Hopkins University Press 2008, pp.29–44, quotation from p.89.
4. John Milbank, *The Word Made Strange: Theology, Language, Culture*, Oxford, Blackwell 1997, pp.18–24.
5. Giles Waller, 'Freedom, Fate and Sin in Donald MacKinnon's Use of Tragedy', in T. Kevin Taylor and Giles Waller (eds), *Christian Theology and Tragedy: Theologians, Tragic Literature and Tragic Theory*, Franham, Ashgate 2011, pp.101–18, quotation from p.113.
6. Milbank, *The Word Made Strange*, p.21.
7. Ibid., pp.22–3.
8. Ibid., p.30.
9. Ibid.
10. Section II, l.114.
11. David Bentley Hart, *The Beauty of the Infinite: The Aesthetics of Christian Truth*, Grand Rapids, Eerdmans 2003, p.386.
12. Ibid., p.384.
13. Ibid., p.386.
14. Ibid., p.393.
15. Ibid., p.377.
16. Ibid.
17. Donald MacKinnon, 'Some Notes on the Irreversibility of Time', in MacKinnon, *Explorations in Theology*, London, SCM Press 1979, pp.90–8.
18. Ibid., p.96.

19. From the earlyish essay on 'Atonement and Tragedy' reprinted in *Borderlands of Theology and Other Essays*, London, Lutterworth 1968, pp.97–104, through to *The Problem of Metaphysics*, Cambridge University Press 1974, especially pp.125–31.

20. MacKinnon, 'Some Notes on the Irreversibility of Time', pp.96–7.

21. MacKinnon, *The Problem of Metaphysics*, pp.137–40.

22. Hart, *The Beauty of the Infinite*, p.393.

23. Terry Eagleton, *Hope Without Optimism*, Charlottesville VA, University of Virginia Press 2015, p.107. Cf. the words of Simon Palfrey, in his brilliantly innovative essay on *Lear, Poor Tom: Living 'King Lear'*, University of Chicago Press 2014, p.44: 'But life must protest [against a teleology of suffering]: on behalf of life, named or not. Tom lives, Cordelia lives, just as Job's slaves and children and animals lived…I want to insist on their lives, and on the grief felt at their going. Perhaps something returns at the work's end: but no them. Some substitutions are not ethical.'

24. Ibid., p.37.

25. Ibid., pp.71–2.

26. See pp.58–9 above.

27. Jeanette Winterson, in her contemporary reworking of the story, *The Gap of Time*, London, Hogarth/Penguin Books 2015, p.287, beautifully sums up this conclusion: 'Hermione does the thing most difficult to do to right a wrong situation: nothing.'

28. The most significant texts are in Balthasar, *The Glory of the Lord, vol. IV. The Realm of Metaphysics in Antiquity*, Edinburgh, T. and T. Clark 1989, pp.101–54, and *Theo-Drama: Theological Dramatic Theory*, Vol. I, San Francisco, Ignatius Press 1988, Part IIB ('Elements of the Dramatic', especially pp.424–51), and Vol. IV, San Francisco, Ignatius Press 1994. There is good critical discussion of the overlaps and tensions between Balthasar and Hegel in Ben Quash, *Theology and the Drama of History*, Cambridge University Press 2005, especially chapter 3.

29. T. Kevin Taylor, 'Hans Urs von Balthasar and Christ the Tragic Hero', in Taylor and Waller (eds), *Christian Theology and Tragedy*, pp.133–48, quotation from p.136.

30. A position usually associated with Jurgen Moltmann; see especially his *The Crucified God*, London, SCM Press 1974, especially chapter 6.

31. The resurrection of Jesus 'is not a descent from the cross postponed for thirty-six hours'; MacKinnon, *Borderlands of Theology and Other Essays*, p.95.

32. Eagleton, *Hope Without Optimism*, p.115.

33. Line 70. Subsequent references are by bracketed line number in the text.

34. *Oedipus at Colonus*, in *Sophocles: The Three Theban Plays*, translated by Robert Fagles, Harmondsworth, Penguin Classics 1984 (revised), l.1999, p.388.

35. Revelation 21.4.

36. Simon Critchley, 'I Want to Die, I Hate My Life', in Felski, *Rethinking Tragedy*, pp.170–95.

37. Ibid., p.171.

38. 'Great Sun, shining creator of a doomed race,
You whose daughter my mother claimed to be,
Appalled as you must be at how you see me now,
Let me look upon you one last time.'
(Jean Racine, *Phedra*, translated by Julie Rose, London, Nick Hern Books 2001, p.14.)

39. Critchley, 'I Want to Die, I Hate My Life', p.176.
40. Ibid., p.180.
41. Ibid., p.181.
42. Ibid., p.188.
43. Ibid., p.191.
44. Quoted in Jennifer Wallace, *The Cambridge Introduction to Tragedy*, Cambridge University Press 2007, p.42.
45. Critchley, 'I Want to Die, I Hate My Life', p.189.
46. Ibid., p.190.

6
Conclusions

I

Throughout this book, we have been noting the risks involved in searches for the 'essentially' tragic. We are not here discussing what would make a painful human experience 'tragic', but whether there are more or less consistent themes running through the particular set of literary compositions commonly referred to by that adjective. Without this caveat, we are in danger of forcing a variety of imaginative productions into a straitjacket—as we saw in looking at the debates around 'absolute' tragedy. Equally, we are not discussing the moral and theological problem of innocent suffering as an abstract question. What I have been calling tragic narrative or tragic representation is not conceived as a response to or resolution of such issues. But—all that being said—it should also be clear that reflecting on the texts identified as tragedies opens up some very broad questions about self and society, and may even have repercussions for our discourses about theology and metaphysics. What we have been tracing is the development of a literary *practice*: tragedy has been something that writers and audiences have *done* in certain social and historical contexts; and they have gone on doing it, and gone on rethinking what they are doing, because the questions with which tragic narrative deals are persistent and difficult and because the way in which tragic narrative deals with them has proved generative of positive insight. In this concluding chapter, therefore, I don't intend to argue that there is a universal, cross-cultural category of experience called 'the tragic', or that there is something called 'tragedy' which poses specific metaphysical challenges to human imagination as such. But I believe that the story of a particular dramatic practice that begins in ancient Athens does generate issues about political philosophy, about selfhood and intelligence, about the possibilities of empathy and the possibilities of hope which are of very broad significance. In other words, if literary tragedy is indeed, as many would claim, the product of an exclusively European cultural history, this does not mean that it fails to raise issues of abiding and general importance and to offer ways of confronting them.

The point is worth pausing on. As a matter of bare fact, what most writers, audiences, and critics mean by tragedy is indeed a phenomenon with a particular local history. We may find analogues for tragic drama in other cultures, not to mention modern examples of tragedy which utilize to powerful effect the collision of cultures as a setting for tragic conflict. It is common to point to the Japanese Noh drama, which developed quite independently of the European dramatic tradition, as a vehicle for exploring suffering, loss, and the memory of unhealed injury.[1] Like classical Greek drama, it is an essentially liturgical proceeding; and in the full Noh performance, a sequence of short dramas in different narrative conventions, telling familiar stories, will be separated by carnivalesque intermissions, not wholly unlike the combination in Greece of tragedy and 'satyr play'. But the parallels must not be stretched too far: Noh drama enacts the very briefest of narratives, in which the recurrent theme is the porous and unstable frontier between the immediate world of experience and what might best be called the 'uncanny'—whether the sacred, in its strongest sense, or the imprint of the traumatic past upon the present. The *shite*, the main actor in the drama, is expected (and trained, imaginatively and spiritually) to be a sort of crossing-point for these different worlds, and as such is required to become radically transparent to the confluence of forces moving between them. It is not a drama about the kind of civic crisis addressed in classical tragedy, nor does it work with what Aristotle understood by recognitions and reversals (though both terms could be used for some aspects of Noh), nor is it directly about the critical reconstruction of images of the self. It poses its own distinct and serious questions; but it will not do to regard it as a variant of or even a parallel to 'Western' tragedy.

To turn to another set of problems about tragedy's 'local' nature, the question of how it works against the background of post-colonial cultural struggle is a complex one. There has been a good deal of discussion about, for example, the work of Wole Soyinka in this connection as an African dramatist making powerful use of indigenous

Yoruba tradition and ritual to develop a distinctively post-colonial and non-European dramatic idiom which still addresses some of the crises recognizable in the 'Western' dramatic convention that goes back to Athens. Tragic representation for Soyinka is about enacting an immersion into what he memorably calls 'the immeasurable gulf of transition',[2] the state of separation between humanity and the divine realm (which in this context includes the ancestors and the unborn), and so it involves the drama of self-sacrifice. But how is this to be enacted in a world in which there is more than one cultural frame of reference? Soyinka has protested strongly against a reading of some of his dramas as primarily about 'culture clash',[3] and his protest is intelligible if all that this means is a dissonance of diverse local habits or even moral codes. For him what is central is the painful, sometimes almost absurd, situation of the traditional ritual agent being frustrated in enacting the sacrificial drama, so that the *tragedy* is not the death itself but the stripping away or perversion of traditional meaning by colonial violence.[4] What is being represented here is not so very far from the deliberate contemplation of possible civic or social or even mythological dissolution that animates so many classical tragedies: what should, what can, we think and feel in a situation where the most decisive markers of shared meaning are no longer clear or even available? But both the idiom and the outcome are importantly different— as we should expect, given the very particular crisis involved in the tension between indigenous and imported cultures and moralities. This is a different matter from the Greek awareness of the fragility of the fact of cultural or civic settlement as such. There is no point in arguing about whether Soyinka has produced a wholly de-Europeanized form of tragic drama (and, from another perspective, debate contin- ues among his own Nigerian compatriots about whether he has over-essentialized the Yoruba imagination); the point is that he has created a style of dramatic reflection that is a serious interlocutor for the Western tradition, presenting alternative modes of approaching the questions of selfhood, liberty, and the sacred. Despite his personal agnosticism, Soyinka makes constructive use of Yoruba myth and ritual in interpreting the role of the tragic protagonist in terms of the journey of the god Ogun through the chaos that stands between the world and the sacred realm, battling across this gulf in order finally to be dismembered and absorbed into the earth, for the life of the world. It is another telling instance of a dramatic representation which does not assume that there is something improper about affirming a future beyond the dissolution and collapse that is enacted in the drama.[5]

The use of actual classical Western texts in post-colonial settings is another issue again, and one that deserves a fuller treatment in its own right. Kevin Wetmore's analysis of this notes the distinction between appropriations of classical texts in a non-Western context ('re-staging', as it were, in different cultural clothing) and reworkings of the themes to bring out new kinds of tension—ironic appropriations, in the sense that they are vehicles for the critique of conventional attitudes to the Western canon.[6] Athol Fugard's *The Island* (1973) is a drama involving the performance or, better, re-creation, of *Antigone* by prisoners on Robben Island in South Africa's apartheid era, and it is often—justifiably—regarded as a particularly strong adaptation of the Western text, allowing its characters both to articulate their suspicion of the hegemonic Western canon and to rediscover its resources. Other adaptations of the Antigone story have been made (Femi Osofisan's *Tegonni: an African Antigone* has been the subject of a good deal of critical discussion[7]); but there are also significant voices arguing that a fully post-colonial appropriation would have to question much more closely the way these versions (Fugard's included) simply reproduce the polarities of their Western prototypes rather than beginning from the actuality of the current political experience.[8] A properly critical reworking would go further than what I have called re-staging; Fugard's conclusion in *The Island*, which might appear to endorse a resolution in terms primarily of *accepting* an inhuman fate, can be read as a subtle collusion with the violence it seeks to resist, or as a submission to precisely the Western claims of universal interpretative privilege and cultural superiority that have helped to rationalize the very injustices castigated in the text. And, in the light of our earlier discussion of *Antigone*, it is notable that both Fugard and Osofisan in effect treat the play as a *Trauerspiel*, a drama of martyrdom. It might be that a closer reading of the Greek text would allow a more nuanced reworking than this; the *Trauerspiel*, after all, is arguably more culture-specific than the classical tragedy, in its connection to an early modern picture of selfhood and the conflict between principled individual and pragmatic or tyrannical collective.

In the light of all this, we need to be clear about one or two basic points. The idea that Western tragic drama, specifically Greek tragedy, is simply of timeless relevance and universal superiority is one that is very properly challenged by critics and others who are aware of the toxic effects such an assumption may have for our understanding of different cultures. But recognizing this does not give us an excuse for avoiding the question of what exactly it is in this dramatic tradition that makes it more than a simply local phenomenon of culturally restricted interest. Just as with Shakespeare or Dante, the interesting questions are to do with how the text generates unexpected new readings, both in our own continuing reappropriation of it, and in its encounter with different—and difficult—cultural environments. It is as these are worked through that we understand what might be meant by ascribing to a text the capacity to 'transcend' its cultural origins; which is rather different from beginning with the assumption that it is universally authoritative and illuminating as it stands. It 'stands', after all, as a text for *performance*, and performance is always local and material. As we have seen, the Western tragic tradition is born out of highly specific political and social constraints, and it provokes questions from *within* that history, not from some eternal hermeneutical otherworld. We arrive at a sense of what might constitute 'tragic' imagination and representation only by reading, hearing, watching the particular dramatic processes that have generally been given the name of tragedy and registering the specific challenges that these works pose for us in another locality. And it is in accord with that labour of *specific* reading and attention that we can also say something positive about the wider pertinence of tragic texts. How far the 'us' just mentioned is culturally restricted is not something that can be settled independently of the continuing encounter between actual cultures and the way in which *specific* conversations unfold. Only in the ongoing history of performances can there come into existence a 'we' that is more than culturally circumscribed. And it is neither vacuous nor imperialistic to try and understand this encounter in the belief that the tragic tradition has indeed provoked fundamental reflections on human self-awareness and human community, and may still do so. Such confidence does not foreclose the question of what reflections are provoked elsewhere, by other literary or dramatic conventions, or what may emerge in the moment when a culturally specific tradition engages with and is engaged by other voices. But the history of the reception of tragic drama suggests that its capacity to prompt serious reflection outside its cultural homeland is more than a politically convenient superstition.

Which is a long-winded way of saying that being conscious of cultural diversity and properly suspicious of claims to cultural hegemony should not paralyse us—'us' as the modern Western audience for tragedy—in our attempts to grasp what the central moral and political questions are that tragic representation puts to us. It is a fallacy to think that cultural diversity entails a degree of value relativism that rules out trying to formulate questions and perspectives that are more than local and tribal. And what has emerged so far in this book is a set or sequence of questions that have a good claim to be seen as more than local.

(i) First, there is the issue of what it is that social order leaves out: the settled life of human communities necessarily sets bounds to the spiralling patterns of violent competition that culture generates, and it does so regularly by the mechanisms of expelling and dehumanizing those elements that cannot be accommodated, and the 'Dionysian' storms of desire and ecstasy that flare up around the space of civic virtue. As Gillian Rose insists, law and love alike are complicit in violence of one kind or another. But this does not mean either that we are doomed to the constant return of the utterly lawless, the destructively ecstatic, or that we must struggle to identify and defend a form of worldly, contemporary life that will be innocent of violence. Tragic drama in the tradition that begins in Greece proposes a complex way of handling this. There is a solemn corporate event in which events of catastrophe and disruption are re-enacted. Familiar narratives of terror or failure, of the collapse of civic order and moral stability are retold again and again, as if on the basis that we shall never have found the definitive and exhaustive mode of telling them. We as a community are presented afresh with the flaw that runs through our common life, the price we pay for law; not in order to establish that we are always and inevitably guilty but to persuade us to question our own refusal to recognize the violence we are involved in, and thus our refusal to recognize the humanity of the excluded other. In this process, we are recalled to the common exploration of how a more fully lawful community might come into being—not innocent, not without its historical flaws being still present and at work, but with the possibility of a new level of truthfulness that at least does not lie about the scale of cost and the degree of misrecognition.[9]

(ii) This deliberate inviting of risk and disruption into the community's life, even if only in ritualized form, is thus always an occasion for us to consider what it is that we do not know. It reaffirms the limits of mortal understanding and proposes that this may be a matter of anguish and testing but is not an occasion for panic. Our 'lack of certain access' (Cavell's phrase) to the truth of other agents/subjects and our consequent capacity for violent attempts to absorb the other into our own sameness must be faced; and tragedy announces that facing this will not kill us—while refusing to face it will. We are summoned to the recognition of ourselves in the other: not in a way that guarantees the other's accessibility and familiarity, but as a necessary element in our recognition of *ourselves*.

(iii) And in the light of this, we can see, with Hegel, how tragic representation is a moment in the formation of a genuinely thinking subjectivity (of *psyche*, as Walter Davis says): a self-awareness that is not enslaved to fictions about the self—its independence, its native innocence, its capacity to resolve its traumas by intelligence and good will (or, more simply, suppression)—but understands the speaking and thinking self as *what it is that holds the memory of loss and trauma without collapsing*. It is able to do this in part by its sharing in the corporate activity of narrating and grieving loss, without looking for explanation or consolation. In this connection, the Christian activity of representing the most serious possible disruption of what is meant to be ethical and political community— the killing of the human form of God by the process of human law—is a paradigm of tragic performance; the theological context does not evacuate the tragic content and form of the narrative.

In short, then, tragic drama offers both a personal and a political vehicle for absorbing truth and scrutinizing the corporate and individual illusions which define so much of our routine human understanding. What makes the record of appalling pain and loss 'good to tell', in the phrase used by Kathleen Sands,[10] is that this telling locates us in a context of meaning that is both fragile and durable or resourceful. Telling the story of catastrophic collapse is an act of linguistic affirmation: we have not been silenced forever by loss. The irreducible paradox is that in speaking of the worst that can be imagined or experienced, we discover our capacity to 'think' it—not to rationalize or minimize it, but to allow it to pose the question to us: what endures of our humanity? It is tempting to sentimentalize this into a picture of tragedy as a covert celebration of the noble and indomitable human spirit; but this is not at all the point. Tragedy works far more interrogatively and sceptically than that. The moment in *Lear* where the king, faced with the disguised Edgar on the storm-ridden heath, breaks out, 'Is man no more than this?', or the gestures of inarticulate contact and acknowledgement that conclude some of Sarah Kane's dramas are instances of where and how this interrogation comes into focus. Tragic representation is neither a pure statement of the unbearable (whatever that would be; as we have seen, even Steiner is unclear as to what the verbal, let alone dramatic, form of 'absolute tragedy' could be) nor a reassuring coda: it is a way of exploring the question, 'What *follows* and what *follows from* extreme loss?' And however culturally specific the tragic convention is, it would be eccentric to argue that such a question was peculiar to one limited segment of humanity.

II

Several times in this book, mention has been made of 'mourning' as a way of thinking about tragedy. Gillian Rose, in her detailed and seminal discussion of Walter Benjamin, develops Benjamin's distinction between 'mourning' and 'mournfulness' or melancholy—a distinction which is rooted in the argument that what sets ancient tragedy apart from *Trauerspiel* is the focus in the latter on staging a *state of mind*. The equation of tragedy and 'mourning play' is the result, says Benjamin, of '[T]he evaporation of the tragic under the scrutiny of psychology':[11] what gives a drama its status as a *Trauerspiel*, a 'mourning play', is—pretty obviously—its capacity to generate the sentiment of mourning in the spectator. While classical tragedy, in Benjamin's phrase, summons and justifies the audience in the presence of a 'cosmic' transaction,[12] *Trauerspiel* presents a spectacle designed to represent a world that is both structured around states of mind and addressed *to* states of mind. In other words, this kind of drama sets out to create an atmosphere of darkness and sadness, a *mood*, relieved only by the example of stoical heroism. These are plays 'through which mourning finds satisfaction':[13] that is to say, the melancholy subject recognizes the melancholy other; spectator and dramatic agent confirm each other's identity as suffering individuals in a world of absolute power and unpredictable fate. And this is a world radically different from that of classical tragedy; Benjamin argues that we should read Shakespeare as a superior form of *Trauerspiel*; like Hegel, he regards *Hamlet* as the archetypal Shakespearean drama and treats it as a particularly (uniquely?) intensified drama of the individual victim, whose death at the hands of a sovereign and contingent fate makes the play an invitation to reflect on subjectivity and its trials, the modern subject adrift from shared meaning, let alone cosmic meaning. But for classical tragedy, the conclusion of the drama is the end (and the refounding) of a world, a whole polity, a scheme of meaning—not the disaster that overtakes a nobly enduring individual. This latter kind of drama enshrines a world that will *not* either die or live anew.

In the light of this, Rose offers the distinction between 'aberrated' and 'inaugurated' mourning. The argument is complex, but the main relevant point for this discussion is the difference between a mourning that leads to speechlessness and impotence and a mourning that is 'the recovery of strength by moving from refusal of loss to acknowledgment and acceptance'.[14] The former grieves for 'desertion'; the latter grieves for loss which is also the condition of gain—the loss of undifferentiated innocence, of simple unities and convergences, in the negotiation of speech, exchange, historical learning. Rose highlights Benjamin's awareness of the gap between tragedy and 'mournfulness', the psychologizing of disaster, but challenges his failure to clarify the nature of this gap; what Benjamin does not do is to explain the way in which 'inaugurated mourning' resists the temptations of the 'beautiful soul', the refined sensibility that contemplates its own integrity over against a world in which freedom is extinguished. The *Trauerspiel* protagonist confronts a 'death's head', says Benjamin,[15] as 'the form in which man's subjection to nature is most obvious'. There is a gulf between the subject, in whom meaning resides, and the meaningless world, and the only possible mode in which the gulf can be crossed is by 'divine violence', by the apocalyptic arrival of a justice or order so radically transcendent that it cannot be spoken of in advance—revolutionary terror or messianic reconciliation. For Rose,

Benjamin's profound pessimism, what is in effect his acceptance of
the categories of the 'mourning play', leaves him in a place beyond
politics and law. Ironically enough, his analysis of the *Trauerspiel* ends
up in much the same place as the 'absolute tragedy' of Steiner: it simply contemplates the unyielding hostility of the cosmos to human
subjectivity.

And this is what Rose calls '*aberrated*' mourning, grief that is fixed in
itself and for itself, a lament for the way in which the world crushes
meaning; 'aberrated' because distracted from the proper business of
mourning. This is not—in spite of what many have assumed—what
classical tragedy does; it is also not what Shakespearean tragedy does,
whatever Hegel and Benjamin make of *Hamlet*. Classical tragedy, as
we have seen, represents appalling catastrophe in a way that *draws
attention to what it is doing*: it is explicitly acting out what we do not want
to see or know, and thus acting out the fact that what we don't want
to see or know is after all capable of *being* seen and known in some
degree. The horror of what crushes human hope or well-being is a
challenge to thinking, not an abdication from thinking. And *Hamlet*, so
far from being a drama essentially about an individual crisis of conscience is (in a way not that far removed, perhaps, from some of
Soyinka's themes) to do with the violent collision of worlds of meaning, a collision in which significant or legitimate action has become
problematic because of cultural, religious, and political turmoil.
Denmark is a 'city' like Corinth in *Medea*, where public lawfulness is
being dissolved; into this comes the voice of pre-civic justice (revenge).
The real catastrophe of the play is that there is no obvious way either
back to the simplicity of a violent and 'sacrificial' political economy or
forward to restored lawfulness except by the overturning of the state
itself along with the death of the protagonist (who concurs in this
regime change with his dying words). It is not that Hamlet is a character struggling to maintain private integrity in a hostile world; his mind
is a contested moral territory, on whom or on which the diverse threats
to 'lawful', mutual human communication and transaction converge,
with crippling and finally lethal effect.[16] *Hamlet* is not, then, meant to
induce melancholy, or the melancholic contemplation of a noble soul.
Like *Lear*, though in a very different mode, it interrogates the issue of
what we owe to each other; and, like so many classical tragedies, it
examines the cost of being in one way or another shut out of shared

meaning (which is emphatically not the same as being isolated from an essentially arbitrary and meaningless world of power and fate). Stanley Cavell indeed suggests that *Hamlet* begins with 'the refusal and the incapacity to mourn', and that its final business is 'the learning of mourning'.[17] Learning how to mourn is learning how to take one's place in the world:[18] letting go of the ambiguous comfort derived from finding one's identity wholly in the enacting of a father's command, letting go of the refusal to accept a mother's independent sexual desire—these Freudian themes, Cavell argues, shape the drama of Hamlet as a drama of not knowing how to mourn and never—or too late—emerging into the world as an agent. Taking up a position in the world is necessarily losing the position of fantasized security and self-identity that is grounded in the denial of loss.

This is strikingly close to Gillian Rose's understanding of '*inaugurated*' mourning. As she writes in an essay on 'Athens and Jerusalem: a tale of three cities', to claim the right to mourn (as does Antigone) is to claim the freedom to 'carry out that intense work of the soul, that gradual rearrangement of its boundaries'[19] that must follow on the traumatic loss of a loved other, so that the person may return to active participation in the city, with all its challenges to a simple and static integrity. The trauma suffered becomes 'transforming loss'.[20] It is a model that can be extended—as Rose would undoubtedly have wanted—to take in different kinds of loss, not only literal bereavement: the loss of a clear self-image, the loss of apparently straightforward ways of appropriating shared meanings, the loss of civic security, the loss of various sorts of control. In all such situations, the underlying theme is damage and loss of power; and in recognizing the scale and nature of such damage, we let go of the myth of invulnerable inner solidity and so become attuned for that recognition of the complex other, related to herself or himself as I am related to myself—that is, in an evolving pattern of liberty and powerlessness, shared meaning, and threatened abandonment. And for Rose this is ultimately possible in the light of some 'transcendent' conviction about justice or lawfulness: that is, a conviction about how the subject actually comes to a durable and honest condition of awareness, to a 'transparency' to what is the case with the world over and above the specific traumas of our experience. Turning away from denial in the direction of this honesty is the task of inaugurated mourning, loss transformed.

It remains loss; but our representation of it tells us that we cannot live without such loss and that we shall die of denial.

III

So tragic drama is a vehicle for collective mourning; not melancholia, not the apparently dramatic articulating of a schism between self and world—innocent self and meaningless world, vulnerable self and cruel world, or whatever else—but the more complex business of exploring what we have been calling the schisms between self and truth. The self's picture of itself as focal, integral, yet also fragile and abandoned, is what tragedy sets out to dissolve, whether in classical or modern mode. Part of the argument here has been that the sharp disjunction between Greek and 'modern' tragedy, as mapped by Hegel and, in a different idiom, by Benjamin is overdrawn. It is not simply that classical tragedy explores the collision of universal ethical substance and particular human 'misrecognitions', mistaken images of ethical wholeness, while modern tragedy traces the outworking of personal character in event, the reaction produced when fate meets individuality, or something along those lines. If our starting point is—with Hegel—that tragic drama is deeply involved in how we become thinking subjects capable of scrutinizing and challenging our self-representations, there really is a thread running through both Greek and modern, especially Shakespearean, tragic drama. The Athenian tragedy displays the dangers that surround our shared life in the city, dangers for the time being overcome but not definitively abolished by the 'lawful' pattern of civic life. By invoking again the power and seriousness of (Dionysian) non-order, we discover both our fragility and our resources for handling it. The public representation of traumatic pain and disaster may, in Shakespearean drama, be less obviously ritualized and even 'theologized' in any overt way, but it deals with the same deliberate invitation of the destructive into our imagination, individual and collective. We must be induced to contemplate terror and loss of the most extreme kind if we are not to be imprisoned in a moral world that is dangerously shrunken. Thus the desired response to 'modern' tragedy is not the moment of individual identification with the sufferer on the stage, not a moment of simple empathy. In one way, it is a recognition of the limits of empathy: we find that the suffering of others is not to be absorbed into our own feelings. But we also find that the suffering of others is already shared in human communication, *recognized* and named as loss or catastrophe. The audience at a tragic drama, ancient or modern, is being invited to see how suffering is, from one point of view, that which most marks each subject as unique and alone, yet, from another, is precisely 'what we have to talk about'—in both senses of those words. It is what we are *bound* to talk about, if we are not to stop being intelligent subjects; it is the *matter* of what we say to each other, the heart of mutual recognition. Tragedy may at significant moments drive us to silence; it also tells us what there is to speak about.

It is for all these reasons that the discussion in this book has concentrated on drama rather than other representations of pain or disaster. There has been a fair amount of debate as to whether a novel can be 'tragic'; there are some who might argue that the novel is indeed the proper home of tragic narrative in the modern age. It is obviously the case that novels can deal with the kind of narrative that we should otherwise call 'tragic', to the extent that they may invoke extremity of experience, irresoluble moral tension, the dissolution of worlds: no-one is going to deny that Dostoevsky's *Devils* with its 'doubling' of social dissolution with individual collapse or emptiness, its radical challenges to moral foundations, and (in its full version) its uncompromising representation of truly degraded evil (Stavrogin's sexual abuse of the child who eventually hangs herself while he watches through a crack in the door), meets many of the criteria for tragic narrative that we have outlined. The same holds for Thomas Hardy's deliberate reworking of Greek dramatic themes in his novels; or for—say— William Golding's explorations of freedom and nihilism in *Free Fall* and *Darkness Visible*; or Camus's *La Peste* (which deserves fuller reading in tandem with Anouilh's aphorisms about tragedy in his *Antigone*). But the question is not whether fiction is capable of addressing the themes of tragedy, but what it is that distinguishes the dramatic from the novelistic mode, and makes the former arguably prior in importance for understanding the character of tragic representation.

The short answer is that drama compels its audience to share the time its action is taking, and thus, as Cavell and others have stressed, strips us of certain freedoms for that time. As spectators, we are bound to follow the unfolding of the action represented and are prohibited from intervening. We are participants in the action to the extent that what shapes what we see or think or feel during this particular time is what is enacted before us. We cannot turn to the last page or refer back; we can leave, we can break the agreement, but we cannot in any serious way modify the way it works. Of course this is not the whole truth. As soon as there are dramatic *texts*, an individual reader can treat them like other texts, moving backwards and forwards, delaying over a phrase and so on; and once the technology exists to record dramatic performances, we have another kind of 'text' to work with and approach with different behaviours. But the rationale of the dramatic text as such is performance in real time, and it is hard to see how we could intelligibly think of drama in any other way. It is an interesting cultural phenomenon that live broadcasts of stage performances in large venues are increasingly popular; the public deliberately opts for an experience as like that of real-time theatre as possible. Whatever other modes we have of responding to theatrical texts—including the kind of fracturing of familiar texts associated with Charles Marowitz[21]—what remains constant is the necessary absorption of the audience's time into the time of the stage. And when the business of the stage is suffering and loss, I am denied some of the protection or evasions that are normally available to me when I am confronted with these things.

Of course the same is true of what we experience in listening to the recitation of a story; and the earliest liturgical rehearsals of legend or myth in Greek celebrations would have had this character. But—as we saw in our first chapter—what starts off this entire history is the moment when more than one voice is heard on the stage and when dialogical exchange is represented. I no longer simply hear a story; I hear what its protagonists hear, I witness the creation in these exchanges of the conditions for disaster, I am exposed to the potential emotional and epistemological unsettlements that go with this. I/we as audience are immersed in the movement and counter-movement of flawed and dangerous self-representations, the kind of self-representations that—the drama tells us—will lead to mortal danger and hurt. And we are thus invited, to put it no more strongly, to recognize our own propensity for flawed and dangerous self-representation, as individual agents and as societies or cultures or collectives; and so invited to think who we are in new ways. As Julian Young notes in his recent study on *The Philosophy of Tragedy*,[22] intellect as well as emotion is engaged in this kind of drama (what Young calls 'Hegelian' tragedy), engaged inseparably; whereas in—for example—*Trauerspiel* there is not much for intellect to do. What matters with *Trauerspiel* is simply the intense feelings of moral awe and emotional pathos we experience. Young is right to resist seeing tragedy as oriented towards the 'sublime', as so many romantic critics understood it. And to acknowledge all this in tragic drama is not to imply that drama *alone* can invite the unwelcome and subversive knowledge of our flawed self-picturing; it is to note that the way in which we learn this knowledge through drama is one which involves both a bodily engagement and an unavoidable dispossession that in themselves tell us something intrinsic to the knowledge acquired—that we mature in knowing by dispossession of our most immediate and accessible models of selfhood, and that we live in a world of bodily limit (and the attentive mutual negotiation that belongs with this). As we have seen in various contexts throughout this book, drama prompts recognition in a particularly direct way: tragic drama invites recognition of the solid reality of the suffering other, of my own complicity in disastrous misrecognition, of the *self*-misrecognition that intensifies this, and of the way in which suffering and loss are always 'spoken' and contemplated realities before we witness them in this dramatic medium. It is this last point that helps us understand the difference between simply witnessing atrocity, catastrophe, and pain and undergoing the more complex process in which thinking about suffering and thinking about thinking, about the nature of our subjectivity, are woven together. Epic recitation or novelistic narrative will fill this process out in various ways within various cultural conventions; but tragic drama is where we experience the pressure to 'inaugurate' mourning, for each and all of us.

IV

If this is what tragedy does, what relation does it have to what comedy does? Immediately we are confronted with the problem of definition: comedy is a word that can cover a multitude of conventions, from farce or the classical satyr play through parody and satire to 'comedies of manners' and much more. It is not quite enough to say that comedies end happily, though that proved a serviceable enough account for

the Elizabethans. And Aristotle's stipulation that comedy should represent agents 'worse than average'[23]—that is, individuals conspicuously beyond the normal range of variation from the ideal of balance
or beauty—doesn't feel all that comfortable, reminding us of the convention up to and including renaissance drama according to which
physical disability or 'deformity' was automatically assumed to be
laughable. One interesting Hegelian-influenced suggestion, from Mark
Roche,[24] is that comedy is characterized by a more *distanced* contemplation of weakness or failure than tragedy, in that authorial control is
more in evidence: we can see the workings in a different way, as an
author creates coincidence, mockery, and appropriately pain-free disaster. It works with an 'immanent aesthetic', that is, with a world of
reference that is more manifestly the product of authorial will than
tragedy. It is 'answerable' to this frame of reference rather than to any
demands for fidelity to a given set of difficulties generated outside the
drama itself. This is presumably the background of Roche's somewhat counter-intuitive claim that comedy is 'an intellectually more
advanced genre than tragedy':[25] if intellectual advance means a greater
authorial self-consciousness, irony, and control, this could be argued
(though it begs a few—Hegelian—questions about what we mean
by 'intellect').

Roche is right in seeing the common ground of tragedy and comedy as lying in the fact that both present the dissolution of an agent's
selfhood; and we might develop this by saying that tragic self-dissolution directly engages the audience's contemplation of their own
fragility, while the comic variety does not. In comedy, we regularly
begin with characters whose perception of themselves is grossly and
obviously askew; and the unfolding of the action shows how this
misperception is brought to light, with consequences that are both
intrinsically ludicrous and in greater or lesser degree humiliating for
the agents involved. Embarrassment is the key to a great deal (not
all) of comedy, in the sense that the desperate attempt to salvage a
self-constructed identity—or more accurately, reputation—inexorably
leads to a still deeper injury to that reputation: the loss of public face
that a character seeks to escape generates what they try to avoid, and
one of the standard trajectories of comedy is the steady increase of
potential embarrassment. This works both for farce and for less visceral varieties of comic drama. From Feydeau to *Fawlty Towers*, the

driver of farcical comic action is the threat of maximized humiliation as a result of something being exposed that should be concealed; but much the same holds for *Twelfth Night* or *Tartuffe*, and
even a good deal of Tom Stoppard (plays like *Jumpers* or *Arcadia* turn
on various sorts of secrets whose revelation will alter what is possible
on stage). But what makes this different from tragedy is not just that
it is funnier (tragedy can provoke embarrassing or embarrassed or
even intended laughter, as any Shakespearean audience knows), but
that the effect of the self-dissolution represented is limited in crucial
respects. It is not implicated in the collapse of social bonds: comic
catastrophe does not imply or symbolize the ultimate fragility of the
social order. It is set within a pattern of manifestly constructed inci-
dent which points to the controlling imagination of an author. It
uses irony differently from the way it is deployed in tragedy: tragic
irony reminds us of what we as audience know and the dramatic
characters do not, in order to reacquaint us with what *we* do not
know about ourselves and the lethal danger of that ignorance; comic
irony is also about what we as audience know and the dramatic
agents do not, but it moves towards reassuring us. We know, they do
not; the consequence of their not knowing does not threaten us even
if it may both entertain and instruct us. Comic resolution contains
what tragedy allows to spill over; certainly we recognize comic
agents as like ourselves, but what is important is that they are *not* in
fact us. We are left contemplating *them*, not ourselves. And it is not
that this contemplation is necessarily heartless or trivializing. If tragedy tells us that what we don't know will kill us, comedy might be
said to tell us that acknowledging what we don't know *won't* kill us:
the dramatic agents in comedy may be humiliated into a recognition
of their frailty, the frailty of their self-construction, but the plot limits the effect of this to a degree that is something less than fatal.
Comic characters learn how to manage their frailty better, and so
does the audience of comedy. We are made more bold in acknowledging our fallibility by witnessing the way in which discovering
fallibility proves painful but not lethal; but we witness it within a
carefully constructed and limited frame, so that the worst we experience is vicarious embarrassment.

We should not make the mistake of saying in the light of this that
the art-form we call tragedy is innately more ennobling and more

necessary for human flourishing than anything else, especially the art-form we call comedy. It would be more accurate to say that we are dealing with diverse modes of representing fragility and self-dissolution. One of these drives us into thinking what the very nature of our subjectivity is, and the other lets us know that our willingness to embrace this, with the relative loss and humiliation involved, is not invariably fatal: it is possible to see ourselves with something of the ironic distance in which we see the comic characters on a stage, and our personal embarrassment is literally not the end of the world. And just as tragic representation alone might be unmanageably terrifying (hence the satyr plays, or the brief masque at the end of a Shakespearean tragedy), comic representation alone would leave us with, at best, a wry acceptance of the strange contingency of the world, of our vulnerability to chance and our consequent capacity to be ridiculous— not with the knowledge of what damage we can do to ourselves and one another and the bonds of community. Comedy does not press us towards the need for lawfulness and mutuality; as has often been observed, it is in one sense a conservative affair, taking lawfulness for granted. Tragedy is not necessarily revolutionary by contrast (and certainly not 'progressive'), but it obliges us to think through what the absence of lawful mutuality means, and to think about what it is in our self-perception that continues to make lawlessness possible. If we have learned from comedy that we can imagine the dismantling of self-perception without total disaster, we may be able to learn from tragedy that this deliberate entertaining of the knowledge of our fragility is what will protect us in some measure not against suffering and loss but against the terror that loss is necessarily the end of meaning or of hope.

The awkward conclusion that this seems to point to is that the tragic imagination is always framed and informed by the comic. It would obviously be nonsense to say that this comic framing made tragic narrative less appalling. In a sense, exactly the opposite is true. The comic—understood as what tells us that loss can be imagined without total destruction—lets us see *why loss is terrible*. To imagine a wound, you must imagine a body. A scheme in which pain or catastrophe ceases to be shocking is one in which the very ideas of loss or random and unjust suffering lose their intelligibility; but for them to be shocking they must be imagined and spoken of as intrusive, surprising, not 'natural' in the sense of being routinely explicable. This carries the same paradoxical twist that characterizes discussion of the theological problem of evil: we seek an explanation of appalling suffering, but it is precisely the lack of explanation that makes it genuinely appalling. Explanation would allow us to take the focus away from the absolutely specific experience, the particular emotional and imaginative challenge, of pain. It is the *kind* of problem it is precisely because explanation could not make it better. But this is also to say that the specific experience of pain is what it is because we do not take for granted a world in which this is right or inevitable. We look for a world that makes sense not so much of suffering in itself as of the fact that we find suffering an intolerable thing. In such a context, comedy gestures towards the body in which tragedy is the wound.

Which is why neither category will stay still under analysis for very long. As noted earlier, George Steiner concludes a recent essay on tragedy, in which he reshapes and reinforces some of his argument for the impossibility of modern tragedy, with a plea for 'an adequate theory of comedy, of the riddles of grief, singular to man, in the merriment of *Twelfth Night* or the finales of Mozart's *Cosi fan tutte*'.[26] It is a tantalizing way of putting the question—a theory of comedy as a theory of distinctively *human* grieving; and it unsettles his wider argument rather more, perhaps, than he grants. The two examples he cites are telling: these putatively comic works in fact present narratives that deal with deep injuries. They are comic in that they show us human self-delusion indulged and then violently punctured without apparently too many bones being broken. But *Twelfth Night* leaves rather a lot of unfinished business—not only Malvolio's furious refusal of reconciliation, but Sebastian's desertion of Antonio (as the latter sees it), the violent rupture between Toby and Andrew, with the former suddenly and devastatingly breaking out in oafish self-pity and contempt, the bizarreness of the marriages...As for *Cosi*, we are left to imagine how the wreckage will be managed: one couple has been made aware of how lightly emotional commitment can be discarded, the other of a sudden intrusion of real passion that shatters a conventional bond. Is there really a comic 'body' that survives these wounds? Perhaps what Steiner is saying is that comedy which leaves these 'riddles of grief' very visibly unresolved is today the more honest means of representing our human fragility than any effort to recreate a tragic idiom that can never do justice to the sheer scale of atrocity in the twentieth century: if we are looking for representation of our desperate condition, we should abandon the 'eloquence' of tragedy[27] for a more superficially detached or prosaic idiom which at least makes no pretence at rendering what is literally unspeakable and directs our attention instead to the smaller catastrophes of our relations with one another. Whether this proposal is sustainable is none too clear. We could at least observe, though, that it takes for granted a division between suffering that is and suffering that is not 'unspeakable', and thus risks saying that the only pain that can actually be *mourned* is the localized grief of Malvolio or Fiordiligi. But in what sense does such mourning ground our own *thinking of ourselves* when the genre in question is comic—that is, when it does not involve a world's dissolution or an appeal to and for the foundation of law? Are we as comic audience close enough in recognition for this to function in any way as an appropriate carrier of the remembrance of extreme loss? And if extreme loss is not to be 'mourned' in Rose's sense, what are we to do but avert our gaze in one way or another? Which is very much not what Steiner seems to want.

Given that he sees other art forms as handling the extremity of modern atrocity more adequately (Celan's poetry, Primo Levi's prose, film of various kinds), it does seem that Steiner is not exactly claiming that something completely unrepresentable has happened, only that tragic *drama* is no longer the appropriate vehicle for it. We are emphatically not to avert our gaze. But if not, what exactly is the matter with the dramatic idiom we have been exploring? Tragic drama—if the analysis here is correct—leaves us with fewer places to hide than most other conventions; and if there is a chastened and ironic place for comic drama's evocation of 'the riddles of grief', why not the more global challenge of the tragic? The point about 'eloquence' is probably the key issue: does tragedy necessarily involve an untruthful fluency about what is appalling? I don't think this case is made—and Steiner rightly refers to *Woyzeck* as an instance of tragedy that is inarticulate. I suspect that he is still working, consciously or not, with the model that Julian Young calls 'sublimeist'—the notion that tragedy is essentially about human nobility, about 'the experience of a state of being in which one overcomes the pain and finitude of life',[28] and does so in language that is memorable in itself. But we have seen reason to think that this is a misconceived picture of how tragic drama actually works in its presentation of dissolving cities and selves and its implicit insistence that we confront our own dissolution. And since actual tragic drama—as opposed to any supposedly ideal cases that can be adduced—consistently manages this inviting of dissolution in the framework of a continuing shared speech which makes mourning possible, it is consistently pointing (as we noted earlier), not to raw pain, but to losses that are 'told' in a way that recalls us to the unavoidable losses of maturing humanly—not in a way that makes this some sort of justification for pain but as a sheer recognition of what it is to think pain 'humanly'. Distinctively human grief, tragedy in fact is already doing some of what Steiner thinks belongs in a theory of comedy.

So the categories go on shifting and crossing in all sorts of ways. The alarmingly bleak comedy of *Twelfth Night*—echoing similar 'comic' conclusions in other plays, *The Merchant of Venice*, *Measure for Measure*, *All's Well That Ends Well*, and so on—effectively says: here is a restored 'body', a world that has been salvaged from various risks and is now settled through a tidy blend of retribution and marriage; and the price of accepting this settlement is distancing the damage that has been done, not *imagining* (not thinking) the effect of the disruption that has been shown. It is as though this kind of drama points us towards that radically different but inseparable imaginative location where we *can* think the scale of damage. Yet imagining damage in its full and uncompromising reality still requires us to imagine a 'body', a world of just or truthful seeing and mutual recognition that is more than an empty ideal; without this, as we have seen, loss is not really loss. Damage matters; comedy deliberately does not address this, and Shakespeare's ambiguous endings are a way of letting us know that he as dramatist knows this. But damage matters because *what is damaged* or lost or wounded matters, and matters lastingly and ineradicably; tragedy that did not leave us conscious of this 'mattering'—and so of possibilities other than the ones that the drama has enacted—would rob us of proper mourning and so of protest, the 'hope without optimism' that Eagleton explores. Tragedy points towards a comedy that imagines a restored body where the wounds are not ignored or belittled or explained away, healed rather than cured, to go back to Nussbaum's terms. Perhaps the nearest that

Shakespearean drama comes to this is in the ending of *The Winter's Tale*: new life, grief unresolved at one level (because it is still true that there has been mortal damage), the silence of the embrace between Leontes and Hermione, the final plea for more narrative—more drama: 'Each one demand, and answer to his part.'[29]

Talking of the restored and wounded body is of course a nakedly theological metaphor, evoking the wounded and resurrected body of Jesus in the Christian gospels. As we saw earlier, tragedy has a complex but manifold relationship with the Jewish and Christian world of reference, no less than with the Hellenic legacy, a relationship that is not necessarily being loosened with the modern West's cultural drift away from traditional religious practice. The theology of this religious world affirms the existence of a body—an order of relation grounded in the divine, whether the Torah-governed community of the Jewish people, or the 'Body of Christ', that revealing metaphor for the intense mutual dependency and mutual recognition ascribed to the Christian community. It also focuses repeatedly on the catastrophic failure of order in the world, and (especially in the Christian narrative of the dereliction of Christ on the cross) represents the divine itself as in some way wounded, emptied, evacuated of power or evident meaning, in the face of human atrocity. Divine identity no less than human, in this context, comes into our speech and imagining as entailing the enduring of loss; and this inevitably mythic projection of loss into the divine is explored, in Jewish and Christian speculative thinking, as a way of clarifying that the divine is not an inflated version of routine human ego-identity but exists simply as 'bestowal', as an unconstrained giving. Translated into human terms—as it applies, Christianly speaking, to the incarnation of the divine in Jesus and to human beings as followers of Jesus—this establishes the character of divine self-dispossession as the human vocation, but thus also establishes that failure and loss are always there to be confronted in our history; they are not made vacuous or painless by the affirmation that they are sufferings of or in 'the Body' which is the community of grace, but are made speakable and thinkable in that context. They become part of a human culture; which is not a matter of explanation or consolation but simply of connection and recognition.

Various distortions of this subtle balance are familiar in religious discourse—compensatory fantasies, revenge fantasies, moralistic justifications of suffering as 'soul-making' or testing by adversity, and so forth—but the central theme continues to provoke and suggest perspectives. The tragic audience and the critic of tragedy may not share the belief system thus outlined. But, if we are not satisfied with an ideology of tragedy as either absolute speechless despair or edifying affirmation of human endurance, we are going to need an interpretative framework that has something of this theological shape. We need a way of imagining a body whose wounds we both contemplate and recognize, the gravity of whose wounds we are forced to acknowledge. We need to be able to imagine the body—and therefore the city—that will never be other than fragile, threatened by the ignorance of the watching ego, yet never emptied of possibility. The act—the unusual, immobilizing, and receptive act—of watching tragic representation in drama silences certain kinds of fantasy. It isolates us from false and trivializing kinds of solidarity, the collusive togetherness that can be the foundation of corporate violence and expulsion. It confronts us with the intractable otherness of human others, and at the same time obliges us to recognize what it is that allows us to talk with and listen to them. It shows us where and how we might start thinking what the 'self' is. It changes us. You might even say it converts us.

It has a complex and unstable relation with comedy. And we can say this without too much anxiety simply because we are not obliged to identify an essence of 'the tragic', only to notice what happens in this act of witnessing tragic representation, what can be said about the imaginative business of creating and absorbing this sort of dramatic transaction. If it should ever be the case that we come to be 'beyond' tragedy, we should be beyond culture, speech, and hope. Anna Akhmatova's reply to her neighbour in Moscow, which has echoed consistently through these chapters, remains a focal point of definition—not of a tragic 'world view' or any such ambitious and distorting model, but of a particular way of repeating the memory of loss and anguish so that we do not lose the human context of loss, the embodied and specific character that renders it serious and terrible, renders it opaque *and* makes it capable of being shared and thought. And all of this is still said and heard and enacted in the liturgy of mourning that tragedy invites us to make our own.

Notes

1. See Jennifer Wallace, *The Cambridge Introduction to Tragedy*, Cambridge University Press 2007, pp.96–9, for a brief overview; for more detail, Kunio Komparu, *The Noh Theater: Principles and Perspectives*, New York and Tokyo, John Weatherhill 1983.

2. Quoted by Sarah Dewar-Watson, *Tragedy: A Reader's Guide to Essential Criticism*, London, Palgrave Macmillan 2014, p.143.

3. 'The bane of themes of this genre is that they are no sooner employed creatively than they acquire the facile tag of "clash of cultures", a prejudicial label which, quite apart from its frequent misapplication, presupposes a potential equality *in every given situation* of the alien culture and the indigenous, on the actual soil of the latter' (Author's Note in Wole Soyinka, *Death and the King's Horseman*, London, Bloomsbury 2014, p.3).

4. It is significant that in *Death and the King's Horseman* the culturally illiterate colonial administrator (Pilkings) and his wife dress up in a version of traditional ritual garb for a party, to the horror of the local sergeant who protests that it is the vesture of the cult of the dead. Ordered to prevent the ritual suicide of the King's horseman, he replies, 'How can man talk against death to person in uniform of death?' (p.26)—implying that Pilkings is the true agent of death in the situation, the death of meaning. Pilkings's mocking remarks about Christian ritual to his servant a few pages later show that he is equally illiterate in regard to his own culture, his own markers of the sacred.

5. Soyinka's adaptation of the *Bacchae* provides what Jennifer Wallace (*The Cambridge Introduction to Tragedy*, p.90) calls a 'redemptive conclusion', in evoking a kind of eucharistic outpouring of life from the dismembered remains of Pentheus.

6. Kevin Wetmore, *The Athenian Sun in an African Sky: Modern African Adaptations of Classical Greek Tragedy*, Jefferson NC and London, McFarland 2002.

7. Femi Osofisan, *Tegonni: an African Antigone*, Ibadan, Opon Ifa 1999.

8. Extensive discussion in Barbara Goff and Michael Simpson, *Crossroads in the Black Aegean: Oedipus, Antigone, and the Drama of the African Diaspora*, Oxford University Press 2007; Barbara Goff, 'Antigone's Boat: The Colonial and the Postcolonial in *Tegonni: An African Antigone*', in L. Hardwick and C. Gillespie (eds), *Classics in Postcolonial Worlds*, Oxford University Press 2007, pp.40–53. See also Wumi Raji, 'Africanizing *Antigone*: Postcolonial Discourse and Strategies of Indigenizing a Western Classic', *Research in African Literatures*, 36(4) (2005), pp.135–54, a significant critical (in both senses of the word) treatment of both Fugard and Osofisan.

9. Simon Palfrey's *Lear, Poor Tom: Living 'King Lear'*, University of Chicago Press 2014, offers some searching perspectives on this dimension of the tragic imagination.

10. See p.87 above.

11. Walter Benjamin, *The Origin of German Tragic Drama*, introduced by George Steiner, translated by John Osborne, London, Verso 1998, p.118.

12. Ibid., p.119.

13. Ibid.

14. Gillian Rose, *Judaism and Modernity: Philosophical Essays*, Oxford, Blackwell 1993, p.186.

15. Benjamin, *The Origin of German Tragic Drama*, p.166.

16. Julian Young, *The Philosophy of Tragedy: From Plato to Žižek*, Cambridge University Press 2013, p.138, concludes that 'What Shakespeare offers us [in *Hamlet*] is not a discussion of ethics but, as Hegel suggests, a page from a psychologist's casebook.' Only up to a point: this judgement still reflects a vey post-Romantic *Hamlet* (Hegel's *Hamlet*, precisely) in which the inescapable public, political, and theological resonances of the play have been muted.

17. Stanley Cavell, *Disowning Knowledge in Seven Plays of Shakespeare*, Cambridge University Press 1987, updated 2003, p.186.

18. Ibid., p.189.

19. Gillian Rose, *Mourning Becomes the Law: Philosophy and Representation*, Cambridge University Press 1996, p.35.

20. Ibid., p.37.

21. See Charles Marowitz, *The Marowitz Shakespeare. Adaptations and Collages*, London, Marion Boyars 1978.

22. Young, *The Philosophy of Tragedy*, p.268.

23. Aristotle, *Poetics*, translated by John Warrington, London, Dent (Everyman's Library) 1963, 1449a, p.10.

24. Mark William Roche, *Tragedy and Comedy: A Systematic Study and a Critique of Hegel*, Albany NY, SUNY Press 1998, pp.220–1.

25. Ibid., p.98.

26. George Steiner, ' "Tragedy", Reconsidered', in Rita Felski (ed.), *Rethinking Tragedy*, Baltimore MD, Johns Hopkins University Press 2008, pp.29–44, quotation from p.44.

27. Ibid., p.43.

28. Young, *The Philosophy of Tragedy*, p.265.

29. *The Winter's Tale*, 5.3.181.

Acknowledgements

I am very grateful indeed to Philip Davis for inviting me to write this book and for his generous comments and advice on a first draft. Many friends, including current and former students, have contributed greatly: conversations and other exchanges with Christian Coppa, Greg Garrett, John Milbank, Subha Mukerji, Regina Schwartz, and Giles Waller in the last two years have helped immensely to give body to some of the discussions in the foregoing pages. Professor Walter Davis has encouraged me greatly by sending his books and by offering generous support, challenge, and understanding from a very different perspective from my own. I have had the wonderful privilege of twice sharing in a Shakespearean reading weekend at Cumberland Lodge, Windsor Great Park, led by Paul Edmondson, Salley Vickers, and Stanley Wells (with Simon Palfrey as well, at the second of these events, focused on *Lear*). And, as introduction and text will amply witness, friendships with the late Donald MacKinnon and the late Gillian Rose have been abidingly and decisively important in shaping such philosophical perspectives as I am able to bring to bear. Material from chapter 5 was used as the basis for a British Academy lecture in December 2015, and I am very thankful to all those who attended, asked questions, and continued the discussion by correspondence. And my understanding of the theatre has been deeply enriched by conversations over a good many years with Mark Rylance and Simon Russell Beale, as well as by the consistently creative and intelligent questioning of Pip Williams. Thanks to all.

Shakespeare references are to the RSC edition of the *Complete Works*, edited by Jonathan Bate and Eric Rasmussen, London, Macmillan 2007.

Short Bibliography

Apart from the various dramatic texts discussed and quoted, the following books are particularly worth consulting:

Antonin Artaud, *The Theatre and Its Double*, London, Calder and Boyars 1970.

Walter Benjamin, *The Origins of German Tragic Drama*, London and New York, Verso 1998.

Stanley Cavell, *Disowning Knowledge in Seven Plays of Shakespeare*, Cambridge University Press 2003.

Walter Davis, *Deracination: Historicity, Hiroshima, and the Tragic Imperative*, Albany NY, State University of New York Press 2001.

Terry Eagleton, *Hope Without Optimism*, Charlottesville VA, University of Virginia Press 2015.

Rita Felski (ed.), *Rethinking Tragedy*, Baltimore MD, Johns Hopkins University Press 2008.

Christopher Hamilton, *A Philosophy of Tragedy*, London, Reaktion Books 2016, appeared as this book was going to press, and is a valuable new discussion.

G. W. F. Hegel, *Hegel on Tragedy*. Edited and with an Introduction by Anne and Henry Paolucci, (second printing) Westport CT and London, Greenwood Press 1978.

Martha Nussbaum, *The Fragility of Goodness: Luck and Ethics in Greek Tragedy and Philosophy*, Cambridge University Press 1986.

A. D. Nuttall, *Shakespeare the Thinker*, New Haven CT and London, Yale University Press 2007.

Gillian Rose, *Mourning Becomes the Law: Philosophy and Representation*, Cambridge University Press 1996.

Walter Stein, *Criticism as Dialogue*, Cambridge University Press 1969.

George Steiner, *The Death of Tragedy*, London, Faber 1963.

T. Kevin Taylor and Giles Waller (eds), *Christian Theology and Tragedy: Theologians, Tragic Literature and Tragic Theory*, Farnham, Ashgate 2011.

Jennifer Wallace, *The Cambridge Introduction to Tragedy*, Cambridge University Press 2007.

Raymond Williams, Modern Tragedy, London, Chatto and Windus 1966.

Julian Young, *The Philosophy of Tragedy: From Plato to Žižek*, Cambridge University Press 2013.

Index